PSYCHIATRY - THEORY, APPLICATIONS AND TREATMENTS

"PARANOIA OF THE MILLIONAIRE": HARRY K. THAW'S 1907 INSANITY DEFENSE

PSYCHIATRY - THEORY, APPLICATIONS AND TREATMENTS

Additional books in this series can be found on Nova's website at:

https://www.novapublishers.com/catalog/index.php?cPath=23_29&seriesp=Psychiatry+-+Theory%2C+Applications+and+Treatments

Additional e-books in this series can be found on Nova's website at:

https://www.novapublishers.com/catalog/index.php?cPath=23_29&seriespe=Psychiatry+-+Theory%2C+Applications+and+Treatments

PSYCHIATRY - THEORY, APPLICATIONS AND TREATMENTS

"PARANOIA OF THE MILLIONAIRE": HARRY K. THAW'S 1907 INSANITY DEFENSE

EMIL R. PINTA

Nova Science Publishers, Inc.
New York

For permission to use material from this book please contact us:
Telephone 631-231-7269; Fax 631-231-8175
Web Site: http://www.novapublishers.com

LIBRARY OF CONGRESS CATALOGING-IN-PUBLICATION DATA

Pinta, Emil R.
"Paranoia of the millionaire" : Harry K. Thaw's 1907 insanity defense /
Emil R. Pinta. p. cm.
Includes bibliographical references and index.
ISBN 978-1-60876-988-9 (softcover)
1. Thaw, Harry Kendall, 1871-1947--Trials, litigation, etc. 2. Trials (Murder)--New York (State)--New York--History--20th century. 3. Insanity defense--New York (State)--New York--History--20th century. I. Title.
[DNLM: 1. Thaw, Harry Kendall, 1871-1947. 2. White, Stanford, 1853-1906. 3. Nesbit, Evelyn, 1884-1967. 4. Insanity Defense--history. 5. Criminal Law--history. 6. Forensic Psychiatry--history. 7. Homicide--history. 8. Mental Disorders--diagnosis. W 740 P659p 2010]
KF224.T4P56 2010
345.747'02523--dc22

2010001173

Published by Nova Science Publishers, Inc. New York

CONTENTS

PREFACE

On June 25, 1906, Harry K. Thaw, son of a railroad multi-millionaire, fatally shot Stanford White, America's best known architect, during the performance of a Broadway musical. Thaw's motive was a prior sexual relationship between White and Thaw's wife, former model and showgirl Evelyn Nesbit. The trial that began in January 1907—and ended with a deadlocked jury—utilized a temporary insanity defense while drawing on the "unwritten law." It involved some of the nation's top expert witnesses--including four future presidents of the American Psychiatric Association, and a past and a future president of the American Neurological Association. One explanation was that Thaw experienced a "brain-storm" at the time of the shooting, i.e., an "explosive condition of the mind" that caused a temporary defect of reasoning.

The brain-storm diagnosis was ridiculed by the press and public. Experts for the prosecution testified that Thaw had paranoia, considered incurable with treatments of the time. In his closing statements, District Attorney William Jerome argued that "brain-storm" was "the paranoia of the millionaire."

The Thaw trial was the first celebrity trial of the 20th century to utilize an insanity plea. As in other famous cases utilizing this defense, psychiatry itself went on trial. With the Thaw fortune estimated at $40 million, the defense hired the best experts money could afford. The prosecution also had its cadre of noted psychiatrists, leading to a well-publicized "battle of the experts." The strategy for the defense, which consisted of raising doubt regarding Thaw's sanity and generating sympathy for him, proved moderately successful. In spite of a vague meaning for brain-storm and a strict legal test for mental nonreponsibility, the jury did not return a murder verdict. During a second trial, Thaw was found not guilty by reason of insanity.

This book examines events leading to Thaw's shooting of White, and provides details of the trial and testimonies of the principal experts. Drawing largely from psychiatric literature of the early 1900s, Thaw's mental-health history is examined in the context of diagnostic concepts of the time. Possible interpretations in today's nomenclature are presented. *Brain-storm, paranoia,* and *temporary insanity*--and their evolutions in current terminology--are discussed.

With no available trial transcript, details regarding expert testimony were taken primarily from newspapers of the time. The term "yellow journalism," designating sensationalism and an appeal to the emotionalism of readers, was coined in the decade preceding Thaw's trial to describe competitive tactics between newspapers of the day. It is expected that stricter editorial policies of *The New York Times* resulted in more accurate reporting than others papers. Accordingly, the *Times* was a primary source for the preparation of this book. However, it was not immune to journalism bias.

The extensive quotes and details provided by Frederick A. Mackenzie in *The Trial of Harry Thaw* (1928) strongly suggest that he was working from a trial transcript. Because of this and its close proximity to the trial, Mackenzie was a more valuable resource than subsequent books. Of the many later books regarding the White-Nesbit-Thaw tragedy, history professor Paul R. Baker's *Stanny: The Gilded Life of Stanford White* (1989) is the most thoroughly referenced and relied heavily on primary-source material. Consequently, this book was regarded as having more authority than others.

Books written by Evelyn Nesbit, *Prodigal Days: The Untold Story* (1934), and Harry K. Thaw, *The Traitor* (1926), are intriguing because of the principal roles the authors had in events; but they are subject to the writers' recall and are understandably skewed from their points of view. Thaw's *The Traitor* is poorly organized and jumps from topic to topic, sometimes without any apparent connections. However, books by Nesbit and Thaw often do contain information not found elsewhere. As an example, Nesbit, in *Prodigal Days,* described a warm relationship she developed after Thaw's trials with one of the prosecution's experts, Dr. Austin Flint, "spending pleasant hours in his company" in a beer hall.

Very few books, other than Mackenzie, provide details of the testimonies of the expert witnesses. Apparently, expert testimony lacked the luster of other, more lurid, aspects of the trial. Frederick L. Collins' *Glamorous Sinners* (1932) is another exception and provides details of the grueling cross-examination of Dr. Charles J. Wiley by District Attorney Jerome--also mentioning several other experts by name and crediting them (correctly, I believe) with saving Thaw's life. Most books, if they mention expert testimony at all, give it only passing interest and dismiss it and the experts as ineffectual and incompetent. A balanced and thoughtful analysis of the legal strategy in *Thaw* is found in an article by law professor Martha M. Umphrey in *Law and Society Review* (1999).

The author wishes to acknowledge John E. Morcos, M.D., Columbus, Ohio, and Paul T.Omelsky, M.D., Cleveland Heights, Ohio, for their insightful diagnostic comments regarding Thaw's childhood symptoms.

Emil R. Pinta, M.D.
Columbus, Ohio

Chapter 1

THE SHOOTING OF STANFORD WHITE

It was a warm, typical summer evening in New York City on Monday, June 25, 1906, for the opening of the musical revue *Mamzelle Champagne*. The play was held on the roof theater of Madison Square Garden, where patrons could be cooled by breezes drifting amid the city's second tallest building.[1] Stanford White, America's most famous architect, who designed Madison Square Garden, the Washington Arch and other New York landmarks, was in the audience and sat alone at a table always reserved for him [Mooney, 222-227]. Harry K. Thaw, son of a Pittsburgh railroad multi-millionaire, was also present with a group of friends and his wife--former model and showgirl Evelyn Nesbit, at one time considered the most beautiful artist's model in America [O'Connor, 187]. Her looks inspired one journalist to write, "She was, I think, the most exquisitely lovely human being I ever looked at" [Cobb, 199].

Thaw, his wife, and White were no strangers to one another. Nesbit's father died when she was 8, and White befriended her and her mother shortly after their arrival in New York in late 1900. He helped pay for housing and medical expenses and introduced them to influential friends [Nesbit, 5; Baker, 323]. Prior to her marriage in April 1905, Nesbit revealed to Thaw that she was seduced—actually, it was statutory rape--by White sometime in late 1901, when she was 16 years old and White was 47 and married [Nesbit, 51; Baker, 324-325]. She subsequently carried on a cordial relationship with White for

1 Madison Square Garden, at Madison Ave. and East 26 St., opened in November 1891. Stanford White was the chief architect. The tower reached a height of 322 feet, topped by a revolving 18-ft.copper, nude statue of the Goddess Diana. The only taller building in NYC was the New York *World* Building [Roth, 161-163].

several years. After their marriage, Thaw often went into rages regarding White, became obsessed with him, and hired detectives to follow him. Thaw made his wife refer to White only as "the Beast" [Nesbit, 73, 85-86].

During the second act of the show, Thaw left his wife and friends, walked to where White was sitting, and without speaking fired three shots from a revolver into the unarmed and defenseless White. The first shot entered White's left eye and lodged in his brain. The second shot entered White above his upper lip, shattered his teeth and also lodged in his brain. By now White was dead, but Thaw fired a third time with this shot entering White's left shoulder. Thaw calmly walked away, surrendered his pistol and told his wife, "I have probably saved your life." Upon exiting the theater and being arrested, he was heard to say either, "He ruined my wife" or "He ruined my life" [Mackenzie, 30-34].

Chapter 2

TRIAL STRATEGIES AND EXPERTS

The trial that began on Jan. 23, 1907—and ended with a "hung jury"--received worldwide, front-page newspaper coverage and was the first "trial of the century." It involved some of the nation's top defense attorneys, experts and prosecutors. Thaw's father died in 1889 when Harry Thaw was 18, so the Thaw fortune, estimated at $40 million [2], was controlled by Thaw's mother [Mackenzie, 17]. The Thaw family, including Thaw's sister and her husband, George L. Carnegie, nephew of industrialist Andrew Carnegie, hired several of the finest attorneys in the New York area. Former New York Judge William M. K. Olcott and his firm, Black, Olcott, Gruber and Bonynge, were hired to prepare a defense. Another counsel, Louis Delafield, who had represented Thaw in other matters, was also retained [Nesbit, 101].

A specialist in mental and nervous disorders, Allan McLane Hamilton, M.D., an "alienist" in the term of the time, examined Thaw for the defense in the Halls of Justice ("Tombs"). Hamilton, who provided expert opinions in the assassination trials of Presidents Garfield and McKinley, believed Thaw to be insane with a diagnosis of paranoia [NYT 3/1/1907, 2; NYT 3/21/1907, 1; Hamilton 1907]. Thaw's attorneys decided the appropriate defense would be a plea of not guilty by reason of insanity.

Hamilton's diagnosis of paranoia deserves credibility. He examined Thaw four times in the Tombs, the first on June 27th, just two days after the shooting [NYT 3/21/07, 1]. Hamilton also met with a family physician of Thaw's to obtain a mental-health history. A grandson of Alexander Hamilton, he was a

2 In today's dollars (2010), this figure would be approximately $800 million. [U.S. Dept. Labor]. Thaw's father made his fortune as an investor and vice-president of the Pennsylvania Railroad, later diversifying into coal and iron [O'Connor, 193].

respected alienist and a professor of mental diseases at Cornell University.[3] Adolf Meyer, M.D., in his 1928 American Psychiatric Association presidential address, singled out Hamilton as a leading forensic specialist of his time [Meyer 1928]. William Alanson White, M.D., another major figure in American psychiatry, recalled Hamilton as a tall, distinguished and imposing figure [White 1938, 183].[4]

Thaw, however, strongly objected to any notion that he was insane and refused to participate in a defense that regarded his actions as unprincipled or unjustified. He insisted upon a defense utilizing the "unwritten law" [Baker, 385-386].[5] He accused Olcott and Delafield of being in collusion with the district attorney and influential friends of Stanford White to commit him to an asylum.[6]

Thaw managed to convince his mother of the corruptness of his attorneys, and after a brief time she dismissed them. She hired a new team of lawyers at a reported fee of $50,000 [Mackenzie, 20]. The team was headed by Delphin M. Delmas, a famous San Francisco lawyer known as the "silver-tongued spell-binder of the Pacific" and the "Napoleon of the Pacific slope," because of his short stature and many trial victories [Mackenzie, 20; Nesbit, 106].[7]

The "unwritten law" had no legal standing. Texas is the only state during the 1920s to have a specific statute reducing murder to manslaughter for a husband who killed his wife's adulterer, if surprised in the act [Editorial, Yale Law Journal]. The strategy of Delmas would be to establish that Thaw at the time of the shooting suffered from temporary insanity, which robbed him of the ability to distinguish right from wrong. But the argument would also be

---

3 Hamilton had a unique lineage: both his grandfathers had been U.S. secretaries of the treasury. His paternal grandfather, Alexander Hamilton, was secretary under President Washington; his maternal grandfather, Louis McLane, was secretary under President Jackson [Hamilton 1916, 16, 19].

4 Thaw, however, regarded him as one of his "bug doctors" and a "queer person" [Thaw, 153-154].

5 Hamilton withdrew as a defense expert when he learned that Thaw would use the "unwritten law" as a defense, believing this would place Thaw in the electric chair [NYT, 3/1/1907, 2]. Later, Hamilton was subpoenaed by the prosecution and testified "under compulsion" [Hamilton 1916, 399]. Hamilton deserves respect for forming an opinion contrary to the team that retained him, and then adhering to it.

6 Years later, in a peculiar book written by Thaw titled The Traitor (1926), Thaw wrote a long invective of his "betrayal" by a former advocate, presumably Delafield, who tried to have him declared insane, but never identified this individual by name [Uruburu, 304]. Nesbit wrote that the subject of Thaw's title, *The Traitor*, remained a mystery and dismissed his writings as a "meaningless jumble of words" [Nesbit, 165].

7 Delmas was an 1865 graduate of Yale Law School [NYT 3/18/1907, 2]. Born in France, he did not deny rumors that he was an illegitimate son of Napoleon III [O'Connor, 210; Baker, 386].

that Thaw was now sane and did not require asylum treatment. Delmas' thrust would be to attack White's character, emphasize that White had betrayed his trust with young Evelyn Nesbit and taken her virginity against her will; and that these transgressions had reaped humiliation and despair upon Thaw, eventually erupting in Thaw's violent action. The insanity defense would enable Delmas to introduce evidence to make the jury sympathetic to Thaw. Instead of viewing Thaw as an evil-doer, he would be seen as ridding the world of an evil influence [Umphrey]. In essence, it was the unwritten law wrapped around the defense of temporary insanity. One can assume that Thaw was receptive to this strategy that revealed to the world that White was a "beast" and allowed him to walk free.

Opposing the strategy of the defense was the chief prosecutor, William Travers Jerome. Jerome had been district attorney since 1901 and earned a reputation as a formidable enemy of crime and vice, sometimes conducting surprise raids in person on illegal establishments. He boldly fought corruption in the New York City police department and the Tammany political machine [O'Connor; Mackenzie, 21-22].[8]

The defense team hired the best experts that money could afford. Ten alienists were hired at fees said to total $10,000 per day [Mackenzie, 103]. These included three future presidents of the organization now known as the American Psychiatric Association (APA) --William Alanson White, M.D., Charles G. Wagner, M.D. and Charles W. Pilgrim, M.D.; and a past and a future president of the American Neurological Association (ANA)--Graeme M. Hammond. M.D, and Smith Ely Jelliffe, M.D. [Pinta]. Another important witness for the defense was Britton D. Evans, M.D. Evans was an 1885 graduate of the College of Physicians and Surgeons, Baltimore, superintendent of the New Jersey State Asylum at Morris Plains, and a respected and published expert on forensic issues [Polk's; Mackenzie, 110-111].

Among this illustrious group, White and Jelliffe are probably best remembered by psychiatrists today. In 1913 White and Jelliffe founded the *Psychoanalytic Review*, the first journal in America devoted to the psychoanalytic movement.[9] White's 1907 *Outlines of Psychiatry* (New York)

8 Jerome ran unsuccessfully against William Randolph Hearst in the 1906 New York gubernatorial Democratic primary, the governor's race eventually won by the Republican candidate, Charles Evans Hughes. In later years, Jerome made considerable money promoting and investing in the Technicolor process for motion pictures [O'Connor, 320-323].

9 The psychoanalytic movement in America was in its infancy when the Thaw trial opened in 1907. Although Freud had published two of his most influential works—The Interpretation of Dreams (1900) and Three Essays on the Theory of Sexuality (1905)—it was not until

and the White-Jelliffe book *Diseases of the Nervous System: A Textbook of Neurology and Psychiatry* (Philadelphia, 1915)--and their later editions--were regarded for many years as some of the finest texts of their kind [Bunker, 240; Burnham 1983, 64-65]. The elections of White and Jelliffe as presidents of the APA and ANA in 1924 and 1929 reflected the acceptance of the psychoanalytic movement into mainstream psychiatry and neurology [Barton, 111].

At the time of the Thaw trial, however, Hammond was probably the best known of the defense experts. He was an 1881 graduate of New York University Medical College and also received a law degree from that university in 1900. He had been professor of neurology and psychiatry at the New York Post-Graduate Medical School since 1896, and was elected president of the ANA in 1898. He was also known to New Yorkers as a world-class athlete, setting the U.S. record for the quarter mile (54 seconds) during his undergraduate years at Columbia University and breaking the intercollegiate half-mile record [Ackerman; NYT 10/31/44, 19].[10]

The prosecution had its cadre of experts that also included a future president of the APA, Carlos F. MacDonald, M.D., elected in 1913. He was an emeritus professor of mental diseases and medical jurisprudence at Bellevue Hospital Medical College, a consulting alienist at several hospitals, and a former president of the New York State Commission in Lunacy.[11] In 1901, MacDonald had been hired by the defense in the trial of Leon Czolgosz, assassin of President McKinley. He and other experts found Czolgosz sane and rational, essentially eliminating the possibility of an insanity plea [Polk's; MacDonald 1902].

Most of the testimony for the prosecution, however, was provided by Austin Flint, M.D. and William Hirsch, M.D. Flint was an 1857 graduate of Jefferson Medical College, a consultant at the Manhattan State Hospital, and a professor emeritus of physiology at Cornell University [Polk's; Flint].[12] Hirsch obtained his medical degree in 1891 from the College of Physicians and Surgeons, Columbia University, and was also a former professor at Cornell

1909 when he delivered a series of lectures at Clark University, Worcester, Mass., that the movement was said to have come to America. It initially encountered considerable opposition [Wagner 1917; Burnham 1967, 84-123).

10 Hammond was also a national fencing champion, a member of the 1912 Olympic fencing team, and president of the American Olympic Association from 1930 to 1932 [NYT 10/31/44, 19].

11The New York State Commission in Lunacy was established in 1889 to improve care and treatment of the state's mentally ill. Its members were appointed by the governor [Pilgrim].

and a consulting physician at the Manhattan State Hospital [Polk's; NYT 3/16/1907, 2].

Delmas and his team were not in uncharted territory with a strategy that combined the unwritten law with a temporary insanity defense. History professor Robert Ireland reported ten trials regarding the unwritten law from 1843 to 1885, and all had utilized a defense of insanity, often as a means of introducing evidence to make the jury sympathetic to the defendant [Ireland].

The most famous of these trials occurred in 1859 when a team of lawyers that included Edwin M. Stanton, future secretary of war under President Lincoln, won a not guilty verdict for U.S. Congressman Daniel Sickles. Sickles shot and killed Phillip Barton Key, who pleaded for his life, one day after his wife confessed to an affair with Key. Key was the U.S. Attorney for the District of Columbia and a son of Francis Scott Key, author of the words to the "Star-Spangled Banner." The shooting occurred in Lafayette Square, Washington, D.C., within sight of the White House.[13] During the trial, Stanton argued that Sickles was in an "uncontrollable frenzy"—a kind of paroxysmal insanity--and was incapable of controlling his behavior [Spiegel and Suskind]. While not the first time that temporary insanity was used as a defense, as some have claimed [Swanberg, 64], the Sickles case was the first to receive widespread coverage in the press and the first to bring the defense into general awareness [Ireland]. Stanton appealed to the jury's sympathy by drawing on the "unwritten law" with passionate arguments regarding the duty of a husband "to keep his family sacred" and to defend his honor. Without benefit of an expert witness and relying solely upon the observations of a friend of Sickles--who observed him in states of mental agitation and anguish for several days following the shooting--Sickles was found not guilty after only two hours of deliberation by the jury. The usually sedate Stanton danced a jig upon hearing the verdict [Spiegel and Suskind; Swanberg, 66].

However, there were several important differences in the Sickles' case and other unwritten-law trials that made a not guilty verdict in *Thaw* more of an uphill battle. For one thing, the misconduct by White occurred five years before Thaw's attack. It would be difficult to show that the shooting happened in a heated moment brought on by an action that occurred years earlier. And Thaw and Nesbit were not married at the time of her "seduction" by White;

---

12 Flint's father, Austin Flint, Sr., M.D., is the person for whom the Austin Flint murmur of aortic insufficiency was named [Wain, 121].

13 Nesbit wrote that Thaw had considerable interest in the "unwritten law" defense [Nesbit, 93]. In later court proceedings, Thaw compared his shooting of White with that of Sickles [NYT 6/26/12, 9].

and probably had not yet met. Another problem was that New York recognized only the McNaughtan, or right and wrong criteria, for mental nonresponsibility and did not recognize an irresistible impulse, or volitional prong test, as an insanity plea [Keedy 1952].

The irresistible-impulse insanity rule played an important role in previous cases of temporary insanity [Ireland]. This rule in U.S. jurisprudence is traced to *State v Thompson*, an 1834 trial heard in Montgomery County, Ohio [Deutsch, 397-398; Ireland]. The McNaughtan rule, or right and wrong test, derived from an 1843 English trial (although it had been used in England and the U.S. before then) in which Daniel McNaughtan was found not guilty by reason of insanity for shooting and killing Sir Robert Peel's secretary, apparently mistaking him for the prime minister [Moran].

In theory, broader definitions of legal nonresponsibility, such as those that include the irresistible impulse rule, make it easier for the defense to win an insanity verdict. Many psychiatrists—including several founders of the organization that became the APA—favored broad definitions of the insanity defense. Isaac Ray, M.D., in his acclaimed book *Medical Jurisprudence of Insanity* (1838), reasoned that a person should not be criminally responsible if his "mental unsoundness…embraced the criminal act within the sphere of its influence" [Ray 1838, 55]. In an 1847 *American Journal of Insanity* article, editor Amariah Brigham praised those states that had accepted the irresistible impulse as well as the right and wrong tests [Brigham].

At the beginning of the 20th century, 14 states specifically recognized the irresistible impulse rule by either statute or case law. Eight states, including New York, specifically disallowed it. New York, along with Montana, South Dakota and Oklahoma, had some of the strictest statutes, declaring that "an insane person is liable unless he was unable to distinguish right from wrong," and that a "morbid propensity" to commit wrongful acts did not constitute a defense [Keedy 1952]. The "morbid propensity" exclusion disallowed the defense to individuals with uncontrollable impulses or habitual criminal behavior who could distinguish the wrongfulness of their actions [Bouvier, 1055; Eigen].[14]

While in theory stricter legal interpretations of criminal responsibility should make insanity pleas more difficult, actual results in trials may be different. Jurors frequently ignore the finer points of the law regarding legal responsibility and base their decisions on their own concepts of the

14 More recently, the American Law Institute's 1955 Model Law also recommended elimination of the insanity defense for mental disorders "manifested only by repeated criminal or otherwise antisocial conduct" [Finkel, 39].

relationship between mental illness and criminal behavior [Perlin, 577; Finkel, 179]. These concepts are not static and undergo change and refinement during the trial process when there is conflict between the law and jurors' concepts of morality. Law professor Martha M. Umphrey postulated that dialogues between attorneys and experts with opposing viewpoints create a dialectic process that can moderate opinions of jurors regarding legal responsibility, causing doubt and ambivalence that benefit the defense in insanity trials [Umphrey].

Legal scholar Edwin R. Keedy, writing in the 1917 *Harvard Law Review,* realized jurors frequently vote their conscience when he referred specifically to the Thaw case and opined that states with narrow definitions of insanity may make it even more likely for juries to acquit [Keedy 1917]. W. A. White, one of the expert witnesses in *Thaw*, must have recalled the Thaw case when he wrote in 1923 that when negative feelings for the defendant prevail, the verdict will be that he is responsible; but "if sympathetic emotions are more stirred then the verdict is that he is irresponsible, that is insane" [White 1923, 91].

Chapter 3

THAW'S FIRST TRIAL

The prosecution opened and presented its case in just two hours. Assistant District Attorney Francis P. Garvan said the state would prove that Thaw was guilty of murder in the first degree. Witnesses present at Madison Square Garden the night of June 25th were called and gave details of White's shooting and identified Thaw as the shooter. There was never any question that Thaw had committed the act [Mackenzie, 34].

Defense attorney John B. Gleason gave the opening statements for the defense. He said the defense would show that Thaw was not sane on the night of the shooting and believed he was acting in self-defense when he shot White. He explained there were two causes of insanity: heredity and stress. The defense would show there was a history of insanity in Thaw's family and that Thaw had undergone "prolonged stress" regarding White. He indicated that Thaw's symptoms of mental illness began early in life and he demonstrated mental instability since childhood [Mackenzie, 35-42].

The first witness called by the defense was Charles J. Wiley, M.D., former assistant superintendent at the York County (Penn.) Almshouse for the Insane, and a graduate of the College of Physicians and Surgeons, Columbia University [Washington Post 2/6/07, 1]. Wiley had never examined or treated Thaw. He testified that one evening in 1905 both were passengers on a streetcar in Pittsburgh, and he observed Thaw behaving in an "irrational" manner. The motorman had pulled down a window blind so that lights from inside the car would not interfere with his vision. Wiley said that Thaw, without any apparent rational reason, raised the blind, insisting that it remain up, and that he and the motorman became involved in a heated argument. When presented with details of White's shooting in a hypothetical question posed by defense attorney Gleason, it was Wiley's opinion that Thaw was "insane" when he shot White [NYT 2/6/1907, 1-3; Washington Post 2/6/1907, 1].

During the cross-examination, Jerome attacked Wiley's credibility as an expert by having Wiley name neurology texts he had read, and then asking him questions from those texts. He asked him technical details regarding several cranial and peripheral nerves, all of which Wiley answered poorly.

[15] He asked Wiley if he was familiar with the "Argyll Robertson test"[16] (Wiley said he had "seen the name in a book" but did not recall any details), and whether it was named after one or two people (Wiley mistakenly thought it was two) [NYT 2/6/1907, 1-3].

The defense then called two physicians of the Thaw family who had known Thaw since childhood. They testified that Thaw had a "nervous temperament" as a child and that he had St. Vitus dance[17] when he was 6 or 7 years old [Mackenzie, 48-49].

Evelyn Nesbit[18] testified and gave graphic details of her "seduction" by White and the effect this had on Thaw when she revealed it. An estimated 10,000 people crowded streets near the courthouse when she testified. Descriptions were sufficiently lurid that President Theodore Roosevelt and the U.S. Postmaster General explored the legalities of preventing the press from printing future testimonies by her [NYT 2/12/1907, 1-2]. The defense presented her as Innocence defiled, while the prosecution tried to attack her character and reputation in the years preceding the shooting [Mooney, 256-260].

Wagner was the next alienist for the defense to take the stand. He was an 1882 graduate of the College of the Physicians and Surgeons, Columbia

15 Some questions, such as "Does the pneumogastric nerve join the spinal column in the lumbar circle or the dorsal region?" were obviously meant to confuse. The pneumogastric nerve (known more commonly today as the vagus nerve) is a cranial nerve originating inside the skull, not the spinal column [Chusid, 97-98]. Although such questions undermined Wiley's credibility as an expert, they had no bearing on opinions regarding the rationality of Thaw's behavior.

16 A pathologic pupillary response described in tabes dorsalis (a neurologic condition now known to be caused by syphilis) in 1869 by Argyll Robertson, a Scottish ophthalmologist [Wain, 25]. Argyll's brother, Lockhart Robertson, was a British psychiatrist and an early advocate of community care for the mentally ill [Berrios & Freeman, 49-50, 60].

17 St. Vitus Dance (Sydenham's chorea) is an autoimmune complication of streptococcus infection. It causes involuntary movements of the extremities, neck and face, which can be severe. It is self-limiting and not usually associated with long-term neurologic or mental problems [Longe & Blanchfield, 3223-3224].

18 For uniformity, Nesbit's maiden name will be used throughout this book; however, during the years she was married to Harry Thaw from 1905 to 1915, she was Evelyn Nesbit Thaw.

University, and superintendent of the State Hospital for the Insane at Binghamton, NY. He held a faculty position at Cornell University [Polk's; Mackenzie, 103] and was elected president of the APA in 1916.

Wagner testified that he examined Thaw six times in prison. Delmas then read one of the long hypothetical questions that became hallmarks of the trial. Delmas took sixteen minutes to read the question that embodied all the pertinent details revealed so far: Thaw's childhood, his conflict with White, the agony he endured knowing of Nesbit's seduction/rape by White, and the events of the evening of the shooting. It ended with a question as to whether, if the facts of the question were true, the defendant knew that his act was wrong; to which Wagner replied, "In my opinion, he did not."[19] [NYT 2/12/1907, 2].

In future testimonies, Wagner informed the court that Thaw was delusional regarding Stanford White's hiring the notorious New York Monk Eastman gang to kill or "mutilate" him, and about Thaw's previous attorneys (Delafield and Olcott) being in collusion with the district attorney and friends of White. Thaw also informed Wagner that he hired Pinkerton detectives to follow White to get evidence that would put him in prison [Mackenzie, 118-20]. When pressed to state what diagnosis he would give someone with Thaw's symptoms in the annual report of his institution (Binghamton Hospital), Wagner replied that Thaw exhibited "some symptoms" of manic-depressive insanity and some of dementia praecox [NYT 3/20/1907, 2].

The next expert witness to take the stand—and the expert who provided much of the testimony for the defense—was Evans, superintendent of the State Hospital for the Insane in Morris Plains, NJ. The day before Evans' testimony there was a confrontation that set the tone between Evans and prosecutor Jerome. In a corridor outside the courtroom, Jerome refused to shake Evans' hand. When Evans demanded to know why, Jerome replied that he did not believe Evans was a "truth-telling man." Evans was insulted and replied, "You are no gentleman" [NYT 2/12/1907, 2].[20]

It took Evans several minutes to name all the medical societies to which he belonged and the medical articles he had written. He had visited Thaw eight

---

19 "Ultimate issue" testimony of criminal responsibility is controversial today because some consider this to be a moral and legal, not medical, determination [Buchanan]. In 1907 such testimony was allowed, presumably as a result of the 1882 trial of Charles Guiteau for the assassination of President Garfield, where the court ruled that "[if] a witness is competent to give an opinion as to the mental condition of the accused, he is competent to give his opinion...of the knowledge of right and wrong" [Finkel, 64-67].

20 Several years later Jerome was quoted as saying that all the expert witnesses he met during his eight years as district attorney were honest, except one connected with the Thaw case who was "radically dishonest...and you all know whom I mean [Evans]" [MacDonald 1910].

times in the Tombs, six of them with Wagner. The first time he examined Thaw was on Aug. 4, 1906. He noticed "a peculiar facial expression," and "a suspicious manner of viewing his surroundings." Thaw also tried to convince Evans that his previous attorneys had been in a conspiracy with the district attorney's office and with influential friends of Stanford White to have him committed and to keep the truth from the public. He also believed that White hired "thugs" to get him into street brawls, and that he was taunted by these individuals on several occasions. He believed that "Providence [God]" had taken control of him, and that killing White was "an act of Providence." Evans considered this to be an insane delusion [NYT 2/13/1907, 3].

Evans stated that he and Wagner conducted a physical examination of Thaw "from head to foot" that included a complete neurologic examination. They discovered two occipital protuberances, which they regarded as unusual but with no apparent significance. They found hyperactive reflexes, but could draw no conclusions from these findings. They also reported a pulse rate that varied widely. Evans said it was "the most remarkable nervous pulse it has ever been my opportunity to examine." The rate varied from 64 to 112 per minute within very short time-spans. This was checked several times to be certain it wasn't due to the "ordeal of the examination," but each time the findings were similar.[21] The heart examination was normal except for the rapidly changing rate. No physical evidence of drug use was found and no evidence of hypodermic injections [NYT 2/14//1907, 2].

Evans then created a minor sensation when he stated, "I observed a nervous agitation and restlessness, *such as comes from a severe brain-storm*, and is common in persons who have recently gone through an explosive or fulminating condition of mental unsoundness." He explained that in a person with a predisposition to mental illness, the mind can give way due to stress or excitement with a "loss of mental balance." He described this as "an explosive condition of the mind in which the will power is weakened and the reason dethroned—the will power is lost and the person becomes a victim of his diseased condition, operating as a ship does without a rudder in the wind..." [NYT 2/13/1907, 3].

The word "brain-storm" captured the imagination of the public and press, and became a catch phrase for the Thaw trial. Humorists quipped that alienists were now "cerebral meteorologists." Workers arriving late for jobs joked they were delayed by "brain-storms" (Washington Post 3/10/1907, 3). A composer

21 Rapid pulse rate was regarded as an indication of mental disease [Zilboorg 1944, 515]; and German psychiatrist Emil Kraepelin reported hyperactive reflexes and variable pulse rates in dementia praecox [Kraepelin].

of popular melodies capitalized on the term and wrote *Brain-Storm Rag* [Stark]. Evans' name became attached to the term, and future news articles referred to him as the "brain-storm doctor" [NYT 1/24/1908, 2].

The familiar meanings today for "brain storm"--as a sudden idea or inspiration; or examining a problem as a group--were not used until the 1920s [Chapman, 54]. But what was the origin of the meaning used by Evans? Nesbit erroneously credited Delmas with coining the phrase [Nesbit, 112]. Most references, including the *Oxford English Dictionary* [Oxford, 481], credit George M. Gould's[22] 1894 medical dictionary, *An Illustrated Dictionary of Medicine, Biology and Allied Sciences*, as the earliest reference to this term in print: "a succession of sudden and severe phenomena, due to some cerebral disturbance" [Gould 1894, 233]. This meaning continues in modern medical dictionaries, such as Taber's 1993 *Cyclopedic Medical Dictionary*: "a temporary outburst of mental excitement; often maniacal, esp. in paranoia" [Taber, 263]; and in Campbell's 1996 *Psychiatric Dictionary*: "any sudden disturbance in brain functioning" and "bursts of electrical activity within the limbic system" [Campbell, 105].[23]

"Brain-storm" must have been in the medical vernacular before appearing in Gould's 1894 dictionary. In fact, an earlier use of the word in print has been found in an 1879 essay *Are We Automata?* by psychologist William James. James refers to several selves, one of which is the "true Ego" and the other is an "enemy," in which "murderous tendencies" can be kept at bay "until at last the brain-storm becomes too strong for the helmsman's power" [Little]. Evans may have been familiar with this essay because of the use of a similar analogy regarding a "rudderless ship."

Evans continued with his testimony of Thaw's examination. He described Thaw as displaying "logorrhea"—an abnormal and rapid flow of words. He described him as speaking with "ideas lumped one over another in rapid succession" and "jumping from one position to another." He used the phrase "flight of ideas."[24] He also described Thaw as exhibiting persecutory delusions regarding conspiracies on the part of numerous people and considered Thaw to

22 Gould was an 1888 graduate of Jefferson Medical College. He settled in Philadelphia, specializing in ophthalmology, and was instrumental in the formation of the Association of Medical Librarians, serving as its first president [Wannarka].

23 Some writers observed that "brain storm" was very similar to "emotional storm," used by alienists in 1881 to describe Guiteau's state of mind when he shot President Garfield [Somerville]. "Brain storm" was also used by noted British psychiatrist Thomas S. Clouston in 1904 to describe a case of acute mania in a 36-year-old male [Clouston, 179].

24 Both "logorrhea" and "flight of ideas" are generally associated with manic states [Sadock & Sadock Vol 1, 683-684].

have an "exaggerated ego" and "delusions of self-importance." Evans continued, "He believes he is clothed with powers, capacities and abilities…out of proportion of a normal human being." When asked what type of mental conditions these symptoms are usually associated with, Evans replied they could be found in "paranoia" and in "maniacal states" [Mackenzie 110-121; NYT 2/13/1907, 3]. In later testimony, he refused to make a diagnosis saying, "He was suffering from that kind of insanity which rendered him incapable of understanding the act" [NYT 3/20/1907, 2]. Evans also did not believe that Thaw was responsible for his actions the evening he shot White [NYT 2/13/1907, 3].

Jerome then summoned his expert witnesses—termed his "squadron of experts" by reporters [NYT 3/15/1907, 2]. In addition to Flint and Hirsh, these included William Mabon, M.D., superintendent of the Manhattan State Hospital for the Insane; William B. Pritchard, M.D., of the New York Polyclinic Hospital; Allan Ross Diefendorf, M.D., superintendent of the State Hospital of Middletown, Conn.; and Albert Warren Ferris, M.D., of the New York College of Physicians and Surgeons. To save time all were sworn in together [NYT 3/15/1907, 1-2].

One expert called by Jerome was not sworn: MacDonald. MacDonald had assisted the prosecution in preparing its case and was present throughout the trial. He later described an agreement with Jerome not to testify for ethical reasons, because he believed it was not possible to assist with a case and then provide an unbiased opinion [MacDonald 1910].

Flint was the first prosecution expert to take the stand. Jerome first read the hypothetical question previously written by Delmas. Not to be outdone by Delmas, a member of the prosecuting team then read Jerome's version of this question. Perhaps the "monster" of all hypothetical questions, it was 12,000 words long and took one hour and thirty minutes to read.[25] It summarized in detail all the pertinent evidence in the trial to that point. Printed copies were distributed to the other experts. At the end of the long reading, Flint was asked, assuming all facts of the question to be correct, "Did the person described…know the nature and quality of the act and know that the act was wrong?" To which Flint replied, "He did." The other experts sworn in by the prosecution all eventually testified that in their opinions Thaw was able to distinguish right from wrong at the time of the shooting [NYT 3/15/1907, 1-2; NYT 3/16/1907, 2].

---

25 Published in a 39-page, numbered-edition booklet: *The Famous Hypothetical Question in the Trial of Harry K. Thaw for the Murder of Stanford White* by William Travers Jerome (Boehm and Rathbone, 1907).

On March 15, 1907, Hirsch took the stand. Hirsch had read Jerome's hypothetical question and replied that it was his opinion that Thaw knew his act was wrong. In addition to other qualifications, Hirsh informed the court that he had studied in Europe where he had been a close acquaintance of the famous Austrian neurologist Richard von Krafft-Ebing. An English translation of Krafft-Ebing's 1904 *Textbook of Insanity* (F.A. Davis) had been mentioned by the defense to bolster the "brain-storm" theory of temporary insanity. In rebuttal of the "brain-storm" theory, Hirsch stated, "There is no such thing known among scientific men, and there is no scientific sense to be connected with any such term." After several objections, Jerome referred to a case-example from Krafft-Ebing's book that described temporary or "transitory" insanity. This was a 36-year-old woman who became violently excited and "sang songs" for several hours, after which she fell asleep and then awoke completely lucid with no recollection of the event [Krafft-Ebing, 209]. Hirsch was asked if there was any similarity to Thaw's condition, to which he replied, "They are no more in common than a case of smallpox and a broken leg" [NYT 3/16/1907, 2].[26]

The defense next called its expert witnesses in what had become a "war of experts." Earlier a spokesperson for the defense told reporters, "You may be sure that we shall not let Mr. Jerome call more experts than we have done" [NYT 3/18/1907, 2]. The experts were Hammond; Pilgrim, superintendent of the Hudson River State Hospital and president of the State Commission in Lunacy. Pilgrim began his professional career in 1882 at the State Asylum for Insane Criminals in Auburn, New York, the precursor of Matteawan Hospital [Parsons]. He was elected president of the APA in 1910; Menas S. Gregory, M.D., assistant superintendent of Bellevue Hospital; Jelliffe, instructor at the College of Physicians and Surgeons, Columbia University, and a neurology consultant to New York City Hospital; and W. A. White, professor of mental and nervous diseases at University of Georgetown and superintendent of the Government Hospital for the Insane (now St. Elizabeths Hospital), Washington, D.C.[27]

26 In this1904 translation of Krafft-Ebing's book, there is a section on "transitory insanity" that includes "transitory mania." Krafft-Ebing distinguished transitory conditions from other forms of insanity by their duration of a few hours or days. Transitory mania, described as "more like delirium," was characterized by a profound disturbance of consciousness with amnesia for the event that usually resolved after a deep sleep [Krafft-Ebing, 206-10].

27 White had been an assistant physician at the Binghamton State Hospital for 11 years under Superintendent Charles G. Wagner. It was at Binghamton that White first met Jelliffe, who had gone there for several months of study in 1896 [Moore].

All had read the hypothetical questions of Jerome and Delmas and responded to the effect that Thaw was not responsible when he shot White.[28] However, upon cross-examination Jerome had trouble getting the experts to state the form of insanity found in Thaw [NYT 3/10/1907, 2].

Hammond came closest to giving a diagnosis and spoke of "maniacal furor" and "psychokinesia" [NYT 3/19/1907, 1-2].[29] Psychokinesia was a term introduced by British psychiatrist Thomas S. Clouston for states of disinhibition and impulsive insanity [Campbell, 579]. Although not familiar with the term brain-storm, Hammond thought psychokinesia was an equivalent phrase and that both were approximately synonymous with "transitory mania" [NYT 3/19/1907, 2]. Earlier, Wagner also agreed that brain-storm was an appropriate term for Thaw's condition [Washington Post 3/10/07, 3]. During cross-examination, Delmas got Hammond to admit that the classification of mental illnesses was "uncertain" [NYT 3/19/1907, 2].

In his testimony, White stated that Thaw did not have complete knowledge of right from wrong at the time of the shooting, and that his "defect of reason" was consistent with insanity. When pushed by Jerome to state what kind of insanity Thaw had, White responded, "I am not prepared to say." In reference to the cases of transitory mania discussed in Krafft-Ebing, White told defense counsel that the fact that Thaw could recall his actions after the shooting did not discount a diagnosis of insanity [NYT 3/19/1907, 2].

Jelliffe also replied that he had not diagnosed Thaw's disorder. He believed that Thaw was insane and that he had defective judgment "which affected his whole intellectual operations." He told Jerome he did not have enough information for a diagnosis [NYT 3/19/1907, 2]. Jelliffe tempered some of his remarks with sarcasm. Jerome asked Jelliffe if he used anything other than facts in deciding his answers, to which Jelliffe replied, "Yes, I used the letters of the alphabet in framing my answers" [NYT 3/20/1907, 2].

Pilgrim and Gregory also testified that Thaw was legally insane at the time of the shooting. Pilgrim said Thaw believed the act was "praiseworthy." Jerome asked him how that explained Thaw's willingness to go to the police

28 It is not clear how many of the experts actually examined Thaw. Wagner, Evans and Hamilton had for the defense; and presumably Flint for the prosecution. Thaw recalled being interviewed by Hamilton, Flint, MacDonald and Mabon in the Tombs shortly after his arrest [Thaw, 153-154]. One of the purposes of the hypothetical question was that it presented a detailed report of all relevant information, similar to a case study. Opinions were then derived from this material, sometimes without examining the defendant [Stedman et al.].

29 Possibly due to "Freudian slips" of the pen, "psychokinesia" was misspelled in the *Times* as "psychokilesia" and "psychopenesia" [NYT 3/19/1907, 1-2].

station after the shooting. Pilgrim replied he had a "certain consciousness" but not the "correct knowledge of the event." Gregory likewise noted he had an "insane knowledge of the event" [NYT 3/20/1907, 2].

The prosecution then subpoenaed Hamilton to testify. Hamilton had examined Thaw at the request of Thaw's previous attorneys, and believed he had paranoia. Before he testified, Jerome demanded that Hamilton testify regarding all aspects of the case. He informed the court that Hamilton had made a report of Thaw's condition for his prior attorneys, and that this report indicated that Thaw continued to be insane and was not competent to stand trial. He also stated that Thaw's current attorneys knew this opinion. He then stunned most onlookers and Thaw's defense team by questioning Thaw's ability to cooperate with his present counsel. He stated that "not a man" who had watched Thaw's behavior at the trial could believe he was capable of cooperating with his attorneys. *Jerome was now saying for the prosecution that Thaw was insane.* However, he was careful to point out that the inability to cooperate with his attorneys did not make him unaccountable for his actions when he shot White. He referred to a well-know legal case where the defendant was declared insane but capable of distinguishing right from wrong [Mackenzie, 169-171].

After several long arguments, Hamilton was allowed to testify. He stated he had informed current defense counsel that Thaw, in his opinion, was not capable of cooperating with his attorneys, and that he believed Thaw had a form of insanity [paranoia] from which only "two percent might recover." This opposed the defense's strategy of temporary insanity [Mackenzie, 175-176].

Judge James Fitzgerald then obtained affidavits from the expert witnesses for the defense, who all stated that Thaw was capable of cooperating with his attorneys; and from experts for the prosecution, who stated he was not. As a result of these conflicting opinions, Fitzgerald appointed a "sanity commission" to evaluate Thaw's ability of "understanding his own condition, the nature of the charges against him, and of conducting his defense in a rational manner" [Mackenzie, 177-78]. Judge Fitzgerald's ordering of a competency-to-stand-trial evaluation was consistent with requirements today. Several Supreme Court decisions require judges to order competency evaluations whenever they become aware of situations that bring a defendant's mental capacity into question [Mossman et al. 2007].

Members of this commission--two attorneys and a physician--conducted an evaluation of Thaw lasting several days. In addition to Thaw, they interviewed a physician at the Tombs and several chaplains, who had not noticed any irrational behavior on Thaw's behalf. However, some peculiarities were noted such as Thaw's pasting whole chapters of the Bible on his cell walls with marginal notes for his attorneys, as well as scores of newspaper clippings with biblical and literary quotations written in their margins.

The commission also heard testimonies from prosecution experts Flint, Mabon, Hirsch, Ferris and Pritchard who agreed that Thaw had an incurable form of paranoia and would be dangerous to society if released. Flint stated he had "true paranoia," delusions of grandeur, and continued to be controlled by "systematized delusions." *Experts who had at first declared that Thaw was responsible for his behavior were now testifying that he was incurably psychotic.*

Defense experts Hammond, Jelliffe and Evans all testified that Thaw was not responsible for himself when he shot White, but was now able to cooperate with his defense. Evans and Jelliffe went further and stated that he was now normal [Mackenzie, 177-83; Langford, 199-202].

The commission delivered its opinion that "Thaw was a sane man and capable of conducting his defense." Jerome bitterly protested and introduced motions, which were denied, that the opinion of the commission was not binding on the court [Mackenzie, 183-84].

Jerome's strategy to have Thaw declared incompetent to stand trial is puzzling. In many respects, it was a reversal of his previous position. In the course of the competency evaluation, Jerome's own experts testified to the seriousness of Thaw's mental condition. Jerome must have been concerned that jurors would issue a verdict in favor of the defense. Several experts for the defense--especially Evans (despite his maligned "brain-storm" theory)--had presented themselves well in court and made convincing cases for temporary insanity [Collins, 139; Mackenzie, 118]. Also, Thaw's behavior during the trial was at times peculiar and erratic, something jurors would have noticed.[30] The one thing Jerome did not want was for Thaw to be set free. He wanted Thaw confined until competency could be restored; or if found not guilty due to insanity, committed to an institution.

Delmas began his closing defense arguments on April 8, 1907. In his argument he invoked the unwritten law. He portrayed Thaw as a protector of his home and wife: "He struck for the purity of the home, for the purity of American womanhood, for the purity of American wives and daughters." Drawing upon the fact that some experts had not diagnosed Thaw's insanity, he then proposed a mock diagnosis of his own: "It is that species of insanity

30 During the trial Thaw at times appeared very childlike, at one point playing with large bundles of papers he had spread out in front of him. Nervous twitching of his face and a lack of expression were also noted [NYT 3/1/1907, 1].

which, if you desire to give it a name, I will ask you to label it *dementia Americana*...that species of insanity which makes every home sacred...the honor of his wife sacred... [and] whoever stains the virtue of that wife, has forfeited the protection of human laws..." [Mackenzie 184-92].

Delmas, of course, was not suggesting *dementia Americana* as an actual diagnosis. He was hoping that jurors would see a common, universal motive for Thaw's acts—resulting in sympathy for him. Delmas never aggressively argued for an insanity verdict. The jurors had several verdicts they could return: murder in first or second degree, manslaughter, justifiable homicide, not guilty, or not guilty by reason of insanity [Mackenzie, 194].

In his closing arguments, Jerome told jurors, "Justifiable homicide did not mean *dementia Americana.*" He explained that justifiable homicide meant self-defense, not shooting a defenseless person as Thaw had done. Jerome pushed for murder in the first degree. Every act done by Thaw that evening "was the act of sanity," he declared. White's acts were those of "unchastity," not "brutality," and did not justify murder. He then attacked the notion of a "brain storm," calling it "*the paranoia of the millionaire.*" He explained, "If the only thing that lies between a citizen and his enemy is a brain-storm, then...every man had better pack a gun and have the first brain-storm" [Mackenzie, 193-202].

In his directions to the jury, Justice Fitzgerald explained the plea of insanity. He informed them that the "irresistible impulse" had "no place in the law" of New York. He explained, "If the defendant knew the nature and quality of the act he was doing and knew that it was wrong, he committed a crime." There was a legal presumption of sanity so the burden of proof was upon the defense to overthrow that presumption. He also explained, "If a reasonable doubt exists as to whether the prisoner is sane or not, he is entitled to the benefit of the doubt" [Mackenzie, 203-05].

On April 12, 1907, after a deliberation of 47 hours, the jury announced that it had failed to reach a decision. Seven voted for murder in the first degree, and five for acquittal on the basis of insanity. The trial had lasted 11 weeks and four day. The estimated cost to the state was $100,000 ($2 million in today's dollars); and the cost to the Thaw family was most likely 3 to 4 times this amount [Mackenzie, 206]. Thaw was retained by the county until retried 9 months later.

Chapter 4

AFTERMATH

Following the Thaw verdict, there was an outcry from professional groups advocating for reform of the insanity defense and expert testimony. The legal journal *The American Lawyer* devoted the first part of its July 1907 issue to articles critical of the insanity trial process, referring to "the fiasco of the recent Thaw trial" [Defense 1907].[31] One of the articles was written by Hamilton, the first alienist to examine Thaw. Hamilton believed Thaw was permanently insane and accused experts for the defense (who supported temporary insanity) of selling their opinions in what he called "the present prostitution of scientific testimony" [Hamilton 1907]. Hamilton and several other writers proposed that impartial experts be appointed to examine defendants pleading insanity and that they should be hospitalized for observation [Hamilton 1907; Jacoby 1907]. Other writers, including Evans of "brain-storm" fame, spoke out against the use of long hypothetical questions [Jacoby 1907; Stedman et al.; Evans].

Writing years after *Thaw*, Stanford University law professor Lawrence M. Friedman referred to the opinions of the experts as "psychiatric mumble jumble" [Friedman, 338]. The opinion of New York *Evening World* journalist Irving Cobb was more scathing: "[a] scurvy, sweated smear of pseudo-scientific poppycock" [Cobb, 230].

White and Evans believed that some of the strongest criticism by colleagues was created by professional jealousy from those who were not chosen to be experts, or did not receive significant remuneration for

31 Similar outcries by the public and press followed insanity acquittals in the well-known trials of Daniel McNaughtan [Moran, 19-21], Daniel Sickles [Speigel & Suskind] and John W. Hinckley, Jr. [Caplan, 129-161].

testimonies [Evans; White 1908]. White even offered a psychodynamic explanation "in the language of modern psychiatry" that such critics were displaying a "defense reaction" to spare themselves discomfort from emotions with no other outlet. He thought public dissatisfaction was fostered by inaccurate and false news reports, sometimes with appeals "to the emotions almost to the exclusion of the reason" [White 1908].[32] Evans, of "brain storm" fame, endorsed this view and also emphasized that honest differences of opinions occur among medical men, just as lawyers and judges can disagree about the interpretation of a statute [Evans].[33] In his autobiography, published posthumously in 1938, White wrote he was "pretty well disgusted" with his experience in the Thaw trial, and that the media had made a "Roman holiday" of the event [White 1938, 186-187].

Writing in 1909, John B. Chapin, M.D., superintendent of the Pennsylvania Hospital for the Insane, wrote that disagreement among experts was not necessarily detrimental to the defense. He inferred the Thaw trial when he opined that the main strategy of the defense in pleas of insanity is to create a "battle of the experts," where contradictory testimony creates confusion and doubt among jurors and allows them to acquit in cases where they are sympathetic—"such as the unwritten law" [Chapin]. Although the jurors in Thaw said they paid little attention to the experts, it is likely their testimonies influenced the jurors' opinions in ways they were unaware [Osborne].

While White and Hamilton seemed to have bitter feelings regarding *Thaw* (and Evans developed a tarnished reputation), Jelliffe seemed pleased with at least some aspects of his experience. He welcomed the opportunity to come into contact with leading specialists, and the fee he received enabled him to make a trip to Europe to study with the German psychiatrist Emil Kraepelin and others [Burnham 1983, 47-49].[34]

---

32 Adolf Meyer, M.D., in a 1912 address, also accused newspapers of distorting events in the Thaw case, making reference to "yellow press" journalism [Meyer 1912].

33 In articles by White and Evans from 1908 and 1909, the Thaw trial is inferred but not mentioned by name.

34 After the trial, Jelliffe was retained by the Thaw family and testified at his second trial. However, he stated that he never received any fees following the first trial. In 1932, 24 years after Thaw's second trial, he sued for $10,000 but apparently settled for $750 [Collins, 139; Burnham 1983, 47, 107]. Hamilton also stated that he was paid only about one-third of his agreed fee of $10,000 [Mackenzie, 267-268].

Chapter 5

THAW'S SECOND TRIAL

Thaw's second trial opened on Jan. 6, 1908, and was a much streamlined version of the first. Jerome again was chief prosecutor, but Delmas had returned to California and Martin W. Littleton was appointed chief defense counsel. Littleton was known for his wit and verbal agility. He was best known to the public for nominating Alton B. Parker at the 1904 Democratic National Primary [Mackenzie, 208].[35]

Littleton announced that he would take full charge of the strategy for the defense. In order to save Thaw's life he would need an insanity verdict, but this time without the notion of temporary insanity. (This was essentially the strategy of Thaw's first attorneys, Olcott et al., whom Thaw dismissed in the first trial.) Littleton indicated he would prove that Thaw had been insane for many years, and he would present more detailed evidence of insanity among Thaw's paternal and maternal relatives [O'Connor, 237-239].

This trial was free of the extreme sensationalism that characterized the first trial. Judge Victor J. Dowling announced that counsel had agreed to limit the number of alienists to three for each side [NYT 1/24/1908, 2], eliminating the "war of experts" of the first trial. Coverage was usually relegated to inner pages of the *Times*, instead of the above-the-fold, front-page headlines of the first trial. But the trial made page one, and a throng of people mobbed the courthouse when Evelyn Nesbit arrived to testify [NYT 1/21/1908, 1].[36]

During the trial, more evidence of unusual behavior was brought out during Thaw's childhood. A family nurse testified that Thaw used "baby talk"

---

[35] Parker handily won the Democratic nomination, but was defeated by Theodore Roosevelt for the presidency.

[36] Nesbit reported receiving 122 marriage proposals, providing her husband was given the electric chair [O'Connor, 237].

until he was 7. A teacher described "outbursts" when Thaw was 10 where he would emit strange sounds "like a howling animal" and his eyes would have a "wild, wild look and a downward roll." An instructor of Thaw in preparatory school stated that when Thaw tried to explain a problem he often talked irrelevantly and repeatedly failed to understand directions. He also described poor concentration and an inability to follow ordinary demonstrations in mathematics [Mackenzie, 223-227].

Several European physicians testified who had treated Thaw during his trips abroad. A London physician said he was called to treat Thaw in 1899. Thaw was in "a very excitable condition," had a fast pulse and was talking rapidly. He diagnosed Thaw with "sub-acute mania" and prescribed bromide.[37] Another physician testified that Thaw tried to commit suicide by taking an overdose of poison. This physician lavaged Thaw's stomach and observed him for a day, after which Thaw showed no adverse effects. A third physician testified he had treated Thaw for ten days at his hotel in Rome and diagnosed "mild mania" [Mackenzie, 227-229].

The defense called its three expert witnesses. All had testified in his first trial—Evans, Wagner and Jelliffe. This time all agreed on a diagnosis—"manic-depressive form of insanity" [NYT 1/28/1908, 3]. When asked by Jerome why they did not make this diagnosis at the first trial, the experts replied they had not known the entire history at that time [Mackenzie, 235]. Jerome seemed resigned to an insanity verdict. He never called his expert witnesses and the case closed unexpectedly [NYT 1/29/1908, 5].[38]

The trial ended on Feb. 1, 1908, after 25 hours of deliberation by the jury. The verdict was not guilty by reason of insanity. Thaw appeared visibly shaken and upset by the verdict. Justice Dowling ordered the sheriff to transport Thaw to the State Asylum for the Criminal Insane at Matteawan, near Poughkeepsie, where he remained for the next 7 years (except for an escape to Canada for 18 months) [Mackenzie, 245-247].

---

[37] Bromide is a sedative, not used today because of side effects. Other sedatives at the turn of the century included chloral hydrate, paraldehyde, opiates and Trional (sulfonethylmethane) [Krafft-Ebing, 258-266]. Barbiturates were the newest agents on the horizon. The first of these, Veronal (barbital), was introduced in 1903. By 1913, when White and Jelliffe edited *The Modern Treatment of Nervous and Mental Diseases*, Veronal was regarded as "one of the best effective agents...without unpleasant side effects" [White & Jelliffe 1913, 550; Wain, 328].

[38] These same prosecution experts had signed affidavits at the first trial declaring that Thaw was insane and not competent to stand trial. According to the *Times,* Jerome did not call them because he did not want them cross-examined by the defense regarding these affidavits [NYT 1/29/1908, 5].

Chapter 6

"Paranoia of the Millionaire"

District Attorney Jerome, in his closing arguments to Thaw's first trial, characterized "brain-storm" as "the paranoia of the millionaire." Jerome accused Thaw's defense of buying the opinions of their experts. By maintaining that Thaw experienced a brain-storm, the defense made a case for temporary insanity, which did not require prolonged hospitalization. Several defense experts testified that Thaw's sanity had been restored by the time of the trial. If, however, Thaw received a diagnosis of paranoia (the prosecution's diagnosis in Thaw's competency hearing) lifelong asylum care would most likely be necessary because treatments of the time were ineffective and remissions were rare.

After Thaw's first trial, Hamilton, the first psychiatrist hired by the defense, agreed with Jerome's condemnation of the opinions of the defense experts. In his memoirs, published in 1916, Hamilton elaborated on his denunciation of Thaw's defense in what he termed a "gross illustration of the evils of expert testimony." Hamilton, who had diagnosed paranoia, believed that a lavish use of money had been used to employ "a perfect cloud of so-called experts" with contradictory and worthless testimony [Hamilton 1916, 399; NYT 3/1/1907, 2).

"Paranoia" in 1907

"Paranoia" is derived from the Greek prefix "para," meaning beside or beyond, and "nous," the mind. In the Middle Ages, "paranoia" was used in a general sense for insanity [Wain, 237]. In 1907, at the time of *Thaw*, paranoia was applied to "monomania," a term introduced by Esquirol in 1823 for insanity characterized by a single delusion [Wain, 207]. The hallmark of paranoia became systematized delusions [Gould 1907, 976]. The term "paranoic" was used for individuals with this disorder, and, more colloquially, for those considered "cranks" or odd [Gould 1907, 976.]. Another term for paranoia in Thaw's day was "chronic delusional disorder."

"Paranoia" was listed as a psychotic disorder in the first Diagnostic and Statistical Manual (DSM) of the APA, published in 1952 [DSM-I]. In 1987 it was replaced by "delusional disorder" [DSM-III-R]. The word "paranoid" is used currently in the DSM in *paranoid* personality disorder and schizophrenia, *paranoid* type [DSM-IV-TR].

Referring to paranoia, in 1904 Kraepelin commented: "There is undoubtedly a group of cases in which delusions are the most prominent, if not the only, symptom of the disease. In these cases a chronic, stable system of delusions gradually develops without any disorder of the train of thought, of will, or of action" [quoted in Abbot].

In 1907 paranoia was thought to develop slowly over one's lifetime and to have a chronic course. Individuals with paranoia demonstrated no, or only slight, intellectual deterioration, and frequently had excellent memory regarding dates and sequences of events. Hallucinations were few and usually associated with the nature of delusions [Page; Drew; White 1907, 94-99]. Paranoia was thought to progress through several stages that began with traits of suspiciousness, quarrelsomeness, and where ordinary events took on special meanings and were thought to be directed at the individual. Innocent remarks were twisted to indicate a bias against the individual, and hidden agendas were found in trivial acts of others [Rutter, 98-99]. These progressed to a "stage of persecution," where the affected individual believed others were intent on doing harm. The final stage was one of "personality transformation," with systematized delusions sometimes accompanied by auditory hallucinations [White 1907, 94-99].

"Systematized delusions" were delusions that were fixed, supported by arguments, and acted upon as if they were actual facts. They became assimilated into important facets of the person's life. "Complementary delusions" sometimes developed to reinforce and support primary ones [White 1907, 49; McDonald; Krafft-Ebing, 368-369].

Because there was no intellectual deterioration, patients with paranoia were often capable of continuing their occupations and of being self-supporting. Often their delusions did not become apparent until some asocial act was committed [Abbot]. Once delusions of persecution became entrenched, there was a tendency toward violence, and individuals with these delusions were considered dangerous [Abbot; Flint].

True paranoia was rare. There was a belief that most individuals with this diagnosis would eventually demonstrate features of dementia praecox or other disorders if followed over time. The consensus was that, with rare exceptions, the disorder was incurable and required lifelong institutional care [Abbot; White 1907, 105; Krafft-Ebing, 369; Flint].

"Delusional disorder," today's equivalent term, is also rare, affecting less than 0.1 percent of the population [DSM-IV-TR, 327]. Treatment outcomes today, however, are more optimistic than in Thaw's time. According to some studies, over 70 percent of patients with delusional disorders show significant improvement with treatment [Herbel and Stelmach].

"Dementia Praecox" in 1907

Cases of paranoia needed to be differentiated from "dementia praecox," a term first used in 1857 by the French psychiatrist Benedict A. Morel for a group of disorders that began in adolescence that were also generally regarded as incurable. The Latin term "praecox" means early or premature. This concept was refined in 1896 by Kraepelin to distinguish it from periodic and cyclical forms of insanity, such as manic-depression, which do not typically show mental deterioration [Kraepelin; Campbell, 187]. "Schizophrenia," a term introduced in 1908 by Eugen Bleuler, is similar to dementia praecox but does not imply progressive deterioration nor necessarily onset at an early age [Shorter, 107-108].

The Thaw trial appeared to be the first time that dementia praecox was used in a major trial, and the first time this term appeared in *The New York Times*. As a result of Thaw's legal battles, dementia praecox became entrenched in the vocabulary of the general public [Noll].

As initially understood by Kraepelin, dementia praecox was caused by a degenerative disease of the brain. Heredity played a major causative role, but other causes, such as metabolic conditions, were later considered [Kraepelin; Noll]. Kraepelin described three sub-types of dementia praecox that were closely related: hebephrenic, katatonic and paranoid. Although the progression of the disorder was gradual, acute symptoms could develop suddenly. Delusions were widespread, and hallucinations were almost always present during the course of the illness, with "hallucinations of hearing" the most frequent. Individuals with this disorder sometimes developed lack of interest in their surroundings and "negativism," in which food was refused and behavior became oppositional. In almost all cases, the "train of thought" was disturbed, leading in some cases to loss of coherence and the coining of new words [Kraepelin].

In contrast to paranoia, delusions, when present in dementia praecox, were often "senseless and fantastic" and varied over time in content and intensity. Mood could vary from excited to depressed, but often was apathetic with an "extinction of affection." Ability to work was greatly impaired. Uncontrollable body movements (choreiform and athetoid) sometimes occurred in later stages. Other physical features included exaggerated tendon reflexes, dilated pupils, and a heart rate that was "subject to great variations" [Kraepelin]. Kraepelin initially considered the symptoms of the disorder to be permanent and progressive, but later estimates were that about 4 percent recovered and 13 percent had significant remissions [Sadock and Sadock vol 1, 1170].

Additional features of dementia praecox included "shallow emotions"; delusions that were non-systematized, "ridiculously absurd" or "whimsical"; somatic delusions, such as believing another person's body parts had been substituted for one's own; and delusions of being controlled by outside sources, such as electricity or magnetism [White 1907, 142-145; Abbot; Hill; Page; Drew].

Differentiating between paranoia and dementia praecox of the paranoid type was difficult in Thaw's time [Drew; Page], and remains so today for delusional disorder and paranoid schizophrenia. An additional diagnostic complication was that some authors believed there was a transitional form between these two disorders [White 1907, 94-95].

"Manic-Depression" in 1907

There was a third psychiatric diagnosis in Thaw's day that needed to be considered as an explanation for Thaw's behavior. "Manic-depressive illness" was the diagnosis given by the defense in Thaw's second trial, and was not seriously challenged by the prosecution. At the turn of the century, Kraepelin described manic-depression as a cyclical disorder of mood, with either depression or elation [Shorter, 107]. "Bipolar disorder" is the equivalent term in today's terminology [DSM-IV-TR].

Manic-depression, paranoia and dementia praecox were three commonly considered serious psychiatric disorders without an obvious organic or physical cause. "Organic mental disorders" were those in which there was a discernable physical etiology--such as infection, trauma, metabolic diseases, or brain lesions.

Individuals with the manic form of manic-depressive illness had elated mood, extreme joyfulness, poor judgment, rapid speech and body movements, and "flight of ideas," in which thoughts occurred so rapidly they were difficult to express, making comprehension difficult. Delusions of grandeur and paranoid delusions could occur along with hallucinations. As mentioned, some writers described intense states of agitation that began and ended abruptly, in what was called maniacal furor or transitory mania. Violent behavior could occur during these periods [Krafft-Ebing, 206-210].

During the depressed or melancholic phase, feelings of sadness, worthlessness and hopelessness prevailed and suicide was a possibility. Although recoveries from episodes of depression and mania were expected, the prognosis for the underlying disorder was poor, and subsequent attacks were almost certain [White 1907, 121].

THAW'S MENTAL HEALTH HISTORY

From various sources, it is possible to compile a chronology of Thaw's mental health symptoms. However, not all sources may have been reliable, and this compilation may be inaccurate in many aspects.

A history of mental illness among Thaw's blood relatives was brought out during his legal battles. On his father's side, a cousin died in a mental asylum with a diagnosis of melancholia; and an aunt was hospitalized for insanity with persecutory delusions. Similarly, a paternal uncle was committed with a diagnosis of "hereditary delusional insanity" (paranoia). A maternal uncle committed suicide; another maternal uncle was reported to have been insane from age 5; and a maternal cousin was declared mentally ill after he attempted to kill his mother [NYT, 3/1/1907, 2; NYT 1/14/1908, 2].

In addition to a history of St. Vitus dance (Sydenham's chorea) at about age 7, numerous problematic behaviors as a child were described. These included speaking in a language "of his own" that was "unintelligible" until about age 7; a gait described as "unsteady" and "zig-zag"; emotional outbursts when Thaw was 10 years old in which he emitted strange sounds "like a howling animal" with eyes described as having a "wild look and a downward roll"; and frequent tantrums in which he screamed loudly and threw himself on floors. On his first day of school, he screamed until he was taken home. In his memoirs, Thaw implied there was a cake at home that he wanted for lunch. He was subsequently enrolled in a private school where he created disturbances on an almost daily basis in which he would scream for no apparent reason, crawl under a desk, and refuse to come out. An instructor in preparatory school, when Thaw was 10, stated that Thaw frequently failed to understand directions, and when he tried to explain a problem he talked irrelevantly. This instructor also described poor concentration and an inability to follow ordinary classroom demonstrations. Thaw was described as a morose, brooding, and unhappy child, who was not sociable with other children and displayed little emotional warmth in social interactions [Thaw, 17; Mackenzie, 223-227; Mooney, 82-83].

As a teenager Thaw attended another preparatory school, but became homesick and returned home. He attended the University of Pittsburgh and announced he would study law. However, he did not apply himself and soon quit. Apparently, he was not inclined to apply himself to any task for an extended period [Mooney, 82-83]. As a young man, he attempted suicide by cutting his throat [Uruburu, 192]. Thaw's father, concerned about his son's emotional instability, willed him only a small allowance, but following his death, Thaw's mother capitulated and provided him with substantial stipends [Baker, 331].

Thaw displayed a variety of eccentric and unusual behaviors, which led to an unsavory reputation and the name "Mad Harry." When he was 23 he chased a taxi driver down a street with a shotgun because he believed he had been short-changed by the driver [Uruburu, 189]. On another occasion, he attempted to ride a horse into a club where he had been refused membership. When a shopkeeper angered him, he crashed his car into the store window [Baker, 331]. George L. Carnegie, Thaw's brother-in-law, told Nesbit that the family had known for a long time "that Thaw is crazy [and] belongs in an asylum" [Nesbit, 98].

There was also a decidedly darker side to Thaw's personality. As a young man, he was accused of striping a male hotel employee, beating him with a whip, and then rubbing salt into his wounds. In 1902 he was sued by an 18-year-old girl, who claimed he repeatedly beat her with a dog whip, but she died of other causes before going to court [Baker, 331]. Nesbit also described severe whippings by Thaw--almost to the point of unconsciousness--as punishment for being "impudent" [Nesbit, 60-61; NYT 3/19/1907, 2]. In 1917 he was arrested in Pittsburgh on charges of beating a 19-year-old male into unconsciousness; and in the 1930s he was sued for beating a nightclub hostess [Mooney, 274-275]. During a 1909 sanity hearing, the "Madam" of a New York apartment house testified that Thaw was a regular who, under an assumed name, frequently lured teenage girls, as young as 15, to his apartment under the ruse of interviewing them for the stage, and then undressed and beat them. She claimed to know of over 200 girls that he had whipped and beaten, and then paid handsomely to keep them quiet (NYT 7/29/1909, 1; Nesbit, 109-110). Nesbit stated that Thaw collected drawings of Persian, Turkish and Hindu slave girls, and she discovered a drawing in which he had sketched himself whipping a nude girl [Nesbit, 61, 114].

According to Nesbit, Thaw was obsessed with White and believed that White had seduced every attractive, young girl he met [Nesbit, 68]. Thaw described White as a "ravisher" and "morally perverse." He claimed to know that White boasted of seducing 378 girls [Thaw, 106: Baker, 351]. He threatened to kill Nesbit if she mentioned White by name, and forced her to refer to White only as "the Beast" [Nesbit, 73]. He often went into rages regarding White with little provocation [Nesbit, 49-52].

Thaw seemed to envision himself as a rescuer and savior of the girls he believed White had seduced. One of the reasons he hired detectives to follow White was to obtain evidence against him for prosecution, and to rescue girls White had "ruined" [Thaw, 120-129]. However, it appears that Thaw's detectives were never able to find the evidence Thaw needed for prosecution [Baker, 351-352]. After shooting White, Thaw spread out his arms, making the sign of a cross, as if martyring himself for wrongs White had committed [Baker, 390]. In his will, he assumed the extraordinary responsibility of compensating several women by name whom he believed White had seduced [Baker, 388].

Another peculiarity, according to Nesbit, was that Thaw was obsessed with virginity and had what she called a "virgin complex." Whenever possible, he would stay at hotels, such as the Hotel Virginian, that had the word "virgin" in the name. He later lived in Virginia for a time. When Nesbit and Thaw traveled to Domremy, France, where Joan of Arc was born, he wrote in a guestbook, "Joan of Arc would not have been a virgin long if Stanford White had been around" [Nesbit, preface].

Thaw was also controlling, possessive and most likely pathologically jealous in his relationship with Nesbit. Nesbit stated that Thaw did not allow her to have friends of either sex, unless he approved, and watched every move she made [Nesbit, 53-54]. On occasion, he had her followed by detectives (NYT 3/19/1907, 2).

As brought out in his first trial, Thaw was described by the defense experts as displaying an abnormal and rapid flow of words described as "flight of ideas." Nesbit also reported that when she first met Thaw, he had a "wild look" and talked so rapidly she had difficulty understanding him [Nesbit, 3]. During Thaw's second trial, a physician in London testified he had treated Thaw, who was in "a very excitable condition" and was talking rapidly. He diagnosed Thaw with "sub-acute mania." Another European physician testified he had treated Thaw in a Rome hotel for "mild mania" [Mackenzie, 227-279].

As mentioned, both the defense and prosecution experts (in Thaw's competency hearing) believed Thaw was delusional regarding White. Thaw believed White had hired thugs to kill or "mutilate" him, and believed he was taunted by these individuals and instigated to fight on several occasions. He believed White wanted to murder him and subsequently began to carry a gun because he feared for his life [Thaw, 121-122]. After the shooting, he believed that his attorneys were in collusion with former friends of White to have him declared insane. In his competency evaluation, experts for the prosecution said these represented systematized delusions and were consistent with paranoia.

There is no record that Thaw had prominent hallucinations. The only reference to hallucinations during Thaw's trial was from a jailor who observed Thaw the night of the shooting as unable to sleep because of hearing "little girls screaming." Thaw also complained earlier that evening of hearing girls screaming who were being beaten [NYT 3/19/1907, 2].

A "Psychological Autopsy"

Trying to put these complex symptoms into a diagnostic framework is highly conjectural, and may even border on unethical. Guidelines of the American Psychiatric Association consider it unethical to offer psychiatric opinions of individuals who have come into the public's attention without having performed an examination, and without proper authorization [APA, Sec. 7]. Relaxation of these standards could be expected when applied to situations over one hundred years ago. However, it is a valid point that a diagnosis is not likely to be accurate without having personally conducted an evaluation. These concerns notwithstanding, there is an educational and historical value in attempting to place Thaw's behaviors into diagnostic nomenclatures of his time, and in determining how they might be interpreted today.

DISORDERS OF THAW'S CHILDHOOD

If there is validity to the descriptions of Thaw's childhood, he had a troubled youth and was a very disturbed young man. The descriptions suggest a combination of neurologic and psychologically problems that—at a minimum—would represent a learning disorder and/or attention-deficit hyperactivity disorder (ADHD). Other conditions to be considered are a possible seizure disorder and childhood antecedents of a psychotic disorder, such as schizophrenia or bipolar disorder—or actual childhood variants of these illnesses. It is also possible that some childhood behaviors represented acting-out and oppositional behaviors that were reinforced when Thaw got his way, such as being sent home from school in order to have cake for lunch.

However, another distinct possibility is that Thaw's childhood symptoms represented a pervasive developmental disorder (PDD), such as autistic or Asperger's disorder [DSM-IV-TR]. Children with these disorders can have idiosyncratic speech, awkward gait, poor adaptation to changes, frequent temper tantrums, and do not socialize well with other children. They are also prone to obsessive-compulsive and eccentric behavior. There is evidence that autism-spectrum children as adults have increased vulnerability to mood and psychotic disorders, and, in particular, increased rates of grandiose and persecutory delusions [Clarke et al. 1989; Clarke et al. 1999; Abell and Hare]. Impaired social skills, cognitive difficulties and deficient behavioral controls can also result in impulsivity and criminal behavior [Haskins and Silva]. PDD could explain Thaw's troubles as a child and many of his eccentric and impulsive behaviors as an adult. It might have provided a developmental substrate for a psychotic or personality disorder in later life.[39]

PDD might also explain Thaw's variable heart rate described by Wagner and Evans. There is evidence that individuals with PDD have imbalances in their autonomic nervous system, which controls involuntary physiologic activity, such as heart beat. Specifically, there are elevations in the sympathetic nervous system, which cause increased heart rate. Excitability and anxiety in social situations can also produce rapid changes in heart rates in autism-spectrum disorders. Resting heart rates as high as 160-170 beats per minute have been reported in Asperger's disorder [Rausch et al.; Ming et al.].

Did Thaw have a major psychiatric disorder as an adult in addition to possible PDD?

The evidence seems to support an affirmative answer. Hamilton, the first alienist to examine Thaw, reported that he approached Thaw's mental illness with skepticism. In the course of his examination, this skepticism was swept away, and Hamilton concluded that Thaw had a serious illness and diagnosed paranoia. Similarly, the prosecution experts, who also doubted a major mental illness, became convinced of a mental disorder as the trial progressed and diagnosed paranoia during a competency evaluation [Hamilton 1916, 399; Mackenzie, 182-183].

There were good reasons to support the diagnosis of what today would be called a delusional disorder, persecutory type [DSM-IV-TR]. The delusions regarding White and the conspiracy on behalf of Thaw's first attorneys appeared fixed and systematized. Thaw's behavior immediately after the shooting was also consistent with a delusional disorder. Esquirol described individuals driven to homicide as a result of persecutory delusions. Afterwards, an absence of remorse and a sense of relief and satisfaction were common [Esquirol, 366-367]. Similarly, after Thaw killed White, he said he knew "we were to have peace" and that Nesbit "was safe at last." He predicted they would have "sunshine ahead." Interestingly, the line between hatred and admiration was thin. Thaw described White as a man "of many attractions," who "had his good points," and on the night of the shooting, he prayed for White to go to heaven [Thaw, 150-151].

Thaw's behavior after being charged with murder was also consistent with a delusional disorder. Individuals with delusional disorders lack insight into their illness and frequently insist they are sane. "Feigning sanity" is more common among this group than "feigning insanity." Some individuals with paranoid disorders dismiss their attorneys, as Thaw did, and defend themselves *pro se*, which can lead to disruptive and bizarre behavior in the courtroom.[40] The decision to fire attorneys often occurs when the insanity defense is proposed—as in Thaw's case. Beliefs that attorneys are part of a conspiracy are also common in delusional disorders [Mossman and Dunseith].

39 PDD was not recognized in Thaw's day. However, a French physician in 1906 described children who may have had this disorder, calling it "dementia praecocissima," and regarding it as an early manifestation of dementia praecox [Clarke et al. 1989].

40 One notable recent example is the *pro se* defense and bizarre courtroom antics of the Long Island commuter-line shooter, Colin Ferguson. Ferguson, a 35-year-old black Jamaican immigrant, shot and killed 6 passengers and wounded 19 others in 1993. Ferguson had elaborate delusions and accusations regarding many individuals, including judges and attorneys. He fired his attorneys when they planned an insanity defense. He was found competent to stand trial by experts, one of whom diagnosed a delusional disorder. Ferguson was eventually found guilty of all six murders, and of attempted murder for the others [Bardwell].

Symptoms in support of a diagnosis of schizophrenia (dementia praecox) are less compelling. Thaw's delusions were organized, consistent, and involved situations which can occur in real life--unlike the bizarre and fantastic delusions often seen in schizophrenia. His behavior was goal-directed and there was no apparent deterioration in hygiene or self-care. No other negative symptoms, such as blunting of affect or decreased speech, were evident. Hallucinations, if they occurred, were transient and not prominent. However, interruptions in Thaw's "train of thought" and indications of disorganized thinking were reported. It is sometimes difficult to differentiate the disorganized thinking seen in schizophrenia from that seen in adult PDD, and some cases of autism-spectrum disorder are misdiagnosed as schizophrenia [Clarke et al 1989].

Thaw displayed many symptoms commonly associated with bipolar disorder. He was described as having flight of ideas, rapid speech, and had been diagnosed and treated for "sub-acute" and "mild" mania in Europe. Today this would be considered "hypomania." Bipolar patients can become delusional during manic episodes, and can experience violent and explosive episodes. Thaw had a history of depression and suicide attempts, which occur in the depressed phase of bipolar disorder.

An important differential point is whether Thaw's delusions were present when he was not having an affective episode. If they were present for extended periods when Thaw was in neither a depressed nor elated state, this would argue against bipolar disorder. Therefore, the constant nature of Thaw's delusions seems inconsistent with this diagnosis. It is also possible that Thaw's unusual speech patterns were due to autism-spectrum disorder and mistaken for those found in mania or hypomania. Another possibility is that the episodes diagnosed as "mild mania" were cocaine-induced (discussed below).

However, bipolar disorder remains a possible explanation for Thaw's symptoms. Wagner, a defense expert, when pushed for a diagnosis, testified that Thaw demonstrated "some symptoms" of dementia praecox and some of mania. "Schizoaffective disorder" in current terminology, combining features of bipolar disorder and schizophrenia, is therefore another possible diagnosis [DSM-IV-TR].

COCAINE ADDICTION —A "WILD CARD" IN THAW'S DIAGNOSIS

Nesbit believed that Thaw was a regular user of cocaine. She first discovered a hidden box of needles and a hypodermic syringe while they were traveling in Europe. She also observed numerous red spots over his body that she believed were needle marks. Thaw traveled regularly with a locked box carried by his valet, which included drugs, a hypodermic syringe, and whips. Nesbit eventually came to believe that his glassy eyes, dilated pupils, rapid personality changes and violent outbursts were the result of cocaine use. She also observed excessive sleepiness that she attributed to sedation from morphine, which she believed he injected to counteract the stimulant effects of cocaine [Nesbit, 58, 64, 155-156].

Cocaine-related disorders could account for many of Thaw's symptoms. Agitation, euphoria, anger, sexual excitement and impaired judgment can be seen in cocaine intoxication; and depressed mood and excessive sleepiness are observed in cocaine withdrawal. Cocaine can induce psychotic states with hallucinations and delusions. Paranoid ideation and suspiciousness are often the initial symptoms of cocaine-induced psychosis, and paranoid thinking becomes more severe with continued use. Frequent violence is also associated with cocaine use. An additional diagnostic complication is that cocaine can exacerbate underlying psychiatric conditions, such as bipolar disorder and schizophrenia [Morton; Satel et al.].

It is not possible to determine which, or any, of Thaw's symptoms were cocaine related. Certainly, symptoms of "sub-acute" and "mild" mania described by European physicians could have been secondary to cocaine intoxication. The degree to which Thaw's symptoms were caused by cocaine would have depended on the extent of Thaw's usage, which is unknown. Opposing the theory of cocaine-induced symptoms was that Evans and Wagner found no needle marks or indications of drug use during their six-day evaluation of Thaw in the Tombs [NYT 2/14/1907, 2]. However, physical signs of cocaine use, which can also be taken orally, intranasally or smoked, can be easily missed on physical examination. The extent to which cocaine was responsible for his symptoms is undetermined, but needs consideration as an explanation.

PSYCHODYNAMIC SPECULATION

The ego-defense mechanism of projection is important in the psychodynamics of paranoid pathology. In projection, unwanted and intolerable thoughts are disowned, and ascribed or "projected" to others. Freud described the projection of unconscious homosexual impulses in the etiology of paranoid delusions in the well-known case of Schreber, an individual with dementia praecox of the paranoid type [Freud 1911-1913].

There were a number of classic examples of projection in Thaw's mental history. He believed White wanted to murder him, when it was Thaw who had murderous feelings toward White—that were eventually acted upon. He believed White was morally perverse, when Thaw's sadistic and cruel behavior identified him as perverse. He insisted White was a "beast," but some of Thaw's actions were even more uncivilized. For example, Nesbit learned that in Paris brothels, which Thaw frequented, he was considered one of their most degenerate customers [Uruburu, 195].

There is no reason to believe that Thaw had conscious sexual attraction toward White. However, White undoubtedly had sexual charisma, as evidenced by his numerous liaisons with younger women. This charisma was due in part to power derived from his wealth and position in the upper tiers of society. Accordingly, Thaw's comment regarding White's phallic masterpiece, the Madison Square Garden tower, that "its bigness increased in the darkness," is a "psychoanalyst's delight" [Thaw, 143].

Some of Thaw's anger and rage toward White likely represented what is known as a "King David reaction." However, not all of Thaw's anger was pathologic. White had committed statutory rape of Thaw's wife when she was only 16, and anger and resentment toward White was understandable. But Thaw's hatred of White as a "voluptuary" began even before Thaw met Nesbit [Baker, 330]. White had a reputation for sexual liaisons with young showgirls. Thaw was also a notorious playboy with an eye on chorus girls, the circumstance in which he met Nesbit [Nesbit, 2, 29]. The King David reaction is named after the biblical story of King David and Bathsheba, in which King David was responsible for the death of Bathsheba's husband by deliberately placing him in danger on a battlefield. The King reacts with anger when told the story of a rich man, who took a poor man's sheep, when he had many of his own. King David anger involves a combination of projection, identification and rationalization [Laughlin, 236-249]. Said differently, Thaw unconsciously identified with a part of himself in White, creating a strong negative reaction. The defense mechanism of identification is also evidenced by Thaw's will, in which he seemed to identify with White, taking responsibility for White's behavior by making restitution to women White had "wronged."

Thaw was described as being obsessed with White, and with virgins. He was obsessed that Nesbit might be having clandestine meetings with White, and was jealous and controlling in their relationship. Paranoid and obsessive styles of functioning share many similarities. Individuals in both cases are intensely focused, rigid and hypervigilant. Both are highly concerned about events that often have little relevance to others, and they expend considerable mental energy trying to control events over which they have little command. Persons who are obsessive-compulsive sometimes decompensate in paranoid directions [Shapiro, 54-107].

Thaw's "virgin complex" toward women is suggestive of the "Madonna-prostitute syndrome," a type of compartmentalization of thought and affect sometimes observed in persons with obsessive-compulsive patterns. One group of women, virgins (the "Madonnas"), are seen as chaste, virtuous and uncorrupted; the other group, composed of women of lower morals (the "prostitutes"), are viewed as wicked and perverse. Those in the first group are revered and coveted by men as wives and mothers for their children; those in the second group are treated with disdain, but sought after for sexual gratification. The inability to attach emotions of sex and love to one individual has been termed the "Madonna-prostitute syndrome" [Mathes]. Individuals with this syndrome experience love toward a spouse or a woman who has mothered their children, but are sexually attracted to women of lower morals. In some instances, the "Madonna" may be turned into a "prostitute" by humiliating and degrading her. Freud described a case where degradation of a woman as a love object became necessary for sexual gratification [Freud 1910]. Thaw's whippings of Nesbit may also have represented such an example. Nesbit described Thaw as becoming sexually aroused during whippings, sometimes ending with her submitting to sex, and sometimes followed by Thaw's masturbating [NYT 3/19/1907, 2; Nesbit, 61-62].

Did Thaw Have A Personality Disorder?

Personality disorders are stable, lifelong, maladaptive patterns, commonly beginning in adolescence, which affect thinking, mood, interpersonal relationships, and impulse control. Reality testing is intact in personality disorders. For example, paranoid thinking occurs in paranoid personality disorder, but typically not with delusions, i.e., false beliefs that are not dispelled by rational evidence to the contrary. Individuals with personality disorders sometimes lose touch with reality under stress and decompensate into psychotic conditions.

"Moral insanity" and "constitutional inferiority" were two diagnoses in Thaw's time similar to today's personality disorders.

"Moral insanity" was used by British physician James Prichard in 1835 to describe a condition where there was a "perversion" of natural emotions and feelings (the "moral" aspects of the person) with no hallucinations or delusions and no defects of reasoning (the "intellectual" aspects) [Zilboorg 1941, 417]. Some experts preferred the terms "moral imbecility" and "moral idiocy" to emphasize an arrested moral development [White 1907, 220; Krafft-Ebing, 28]. Krafft-Ebing and others considered moral insanity to have an organic, mainly hereditary, basis [Krafft-Ebing, 622]. "Antisocial personality disorder," in today's nomenclature, is the approximate nosological successor to "moral insanity."[41]

Individuals with moral insanity demonstrated many of the same symptoms found in paranoia, making differentiation difficult. Individuals with either diagnosis were capable of cruel and violent behavior; both could be self-centered and vain; both could appear superficially normal; and both could demonstrate lack of empathy for others. Massachusetts psychiatrist C. A. Drew, M.D., writing in 1904, considered moral insanity and paranoia to be "first cousins" [Drew]. Krafft-Ebing observed that some individuals with moral insanity decompensated into forms of insanity with paranoia [Krafft-Ebing, 625].

There does not appear to be a public record of Thaw's having been diagnosed with moral insanity. However, Thaw demonstrated some or all of today's criteria for antisocial personality disorder. These include failure to conform to social norms, lawbreaking, deceitfulness, impulsivity, and lack of guilt and remorse [DSM-IV-TR].

Thaw was diagnosed with "constitutional inferiority" during his sanity release hearings [Mackenzie, 260, 265; NYT 7/11/1912, 5], a term sometimes equated with moral insanity. However, this term had different meanings at the time of Thaw's legal battles. In 1907, W. A. White described constitutional inferiority as a predisposing factor to mental illness with repeated failures in

---

[41] Antisocial personality disorder, however, emphasizes only one aspect of Prichard's concept—the absence of moral and ethical values. Moral insanity as described by Prichard, Isaac Ray, M.D., and others was a broader concept, and reviewed today would likely include other personality disorders, brief psychotic disorder and impulse-control disorders [Ray 1838, 168-234; Ray 1861].

life and inadequate coping ability [White 1907, 219-220]. Constitutional inferiority was also used as a "catch-all" term in 1905 to describe developmental conditions of uncertain etiologies that did not fall into established groupings—what today might be called "not otherwise specified (nos)" [Meyer 1905]. In a 1907 discussion of constitutional inferiority, Hamilton enumerated symptoms similar to today's "mixed personality disorder," including features resembling antisocial, narcissistic and borderline disorders [Hamilton and Grasset; DSM-IV-TR]. Other writers applied "constitutional inferiority" to individuals with moral insanity and criminal behavior identical to today's antisocial personality disorder [Bryant; Jacoby 1918, 263-266].

Thaw was also diagnosed with an "exaggerated ego" and "delusions of self-importance" [NYT 2/13/1907, 3; Nesbit 166]. Today's equivalent diagnosis might be "narcissistic personality disorder." Individuals with narcissistic personality disorder have a grandiose sense of self-importance, require excessive admiration, lack empathy, are often envious of others, and show arrogant or haughty behavior and attitudes [DSM-IV-TR]. Many aspects of this description are consistent with Thaw's attitudes and behavior.

Could Thaw Also Have Had a Brain-Storm?

Brain-storms could occur in individuals with other mental disorders. Writing in 1910, Philadelphia psychiatrist Frank Woodbury, M.D., opined that brain-storms, a layperson's term, could occur in a variety of psychiatric conditions, including paranoia. Woodbury advised medical experts to avoid the term in the courtroom because it was poorly defined, unscientific, and often a symptom of another, underlying condition [Woodbury].

It is conceivable that Thaw experienced a brief psychotic episode, or brain-storm, on the night of the shooting. Several events came together to create a "perfect storm"—or in this instance, a "perfect *brain*-storm." Prior to going to Madison Square Garden, Thaw had drinks at Sherry's, a famous Manhattan restaurant that had been designed by White's architectural firm. Thaw in the past had refused to be in any establishment that White had a part in building. Later, while he and Nesbit dined at the Café Martin with friends, White entered the restaurant. Although he was not seen by Thaw, Nesbit passed him a note stating, "The B[east] was here but has left." By some reports, Thaw was agitated when he exited the restaurant. While attending the play at Madison Square Garden's roof theater, Thaw sat in the shadow of

White's tower, a phallic representation of White's prowess, where White and Nesbit had intimate encounters in White's tower apartment [Baker, 372-373; Urburu, 272-290].

When Thaw saw White enter the roof theater, it may have provided the final impetus for Thaw's ego to rupture or "snap." Although Thaw appeared rational to many observers, afterwards he strangely gave his name to the police as "John Smith" and identified himself as a student from Washington, D.C. [Baker, 374]. That night in jail he reportedly had hallucinations of young girls being beaten and screaming. These symptoms might have represented a dissociative disorder (a temporary disruption in consciousness or identity) or a brief psychotic disorder, i.e., a brain-storm.

Were the Defense Experts Dishonest and Unethical, as Some Maintained?

The Thaw defense experts were initially criticized for believing Thaw was not responsible when he shot White. They refused to give a diagnosis; or diagnosed a brain-storm--an explanation that was ridiculed in the press and had no acceptance among the prosecution's psychiatrists. As the trial took a number of unexpected twists and turns, they were accused of dishonesty in Thaw's competency hearing for skirting more serious diagnoses, such as paranoia and dementia praecox. Consequently, Hamilton and others accused the defense experts of "prostituting" their opinions. While is not possible to know their reasons, there are other explanations. They may have been motivated by underutilization of the insanity defense; philosophical opinions regarding societal needs for imprisonment and punishment; a moral obligation to keep Thaw out of the electric chair; and they were forced into a dilemma by Thaw's insistence to waive a traditional insanity plea.

Many mental experts of the time believed that laws regarding the insanity defense were too restrictive, and that this defense was not used as frequently as it should [Steadman et al.]. New York had one of the most restrictive definitions of legal insanity, accepting only the McNaughtan right and wrong criteria, and rejecting the volitional or irresistible-impulse prong of the defense. The defense experts were therefore not able to utilize a defense based upon Thaw's inability to resist a violent impulse. Thaw was not agreeable to a traditional insanity defense, and he presumably was competent to waive an insanity plea. He fired his first group of lawyers over this issue, and most likely would have dismissed his second group if they proposed an identical defense. Thaw's team was thrust into a dilemma and perhaps settled for the best defense under the circumstances—a hybrid defense in which temporary insanity was combined with the "unwritten law."

It seems clear that the defense experts did all they could to avoid committing themselves to a diagnosis. Several of the experts, W. A. White, Jelliffe, Pilgrim and Gregory, never did provide one. However, a diagnosis was not necessary under New York statutes. The minimal requirement was to be "of unsound mind" and to have a "defect of reason" that interfered with knowing right from wrong [Mackenzie, 45]. Some forensic experts today recommend avoiding diagnosis in the courtroom because a diagnosis contributes little information relevant to mental responsibility, is often misunderstood by laypersons, and promotes quibbling of diagnostic criteria by the experts [Morse]. When pressured by the prosecution for a diagnosis, Evans and several others gave a layperson's term, a brain-storm, which described certain symptoms, but said little about an underlying disorder.

Another possible reason for their opinions was a belief among some psychiatrists that individuals, in general, did not deserve condemnation and punishment for their actions. Some defense experts, such as W. A. White, endorsed a deterministic philosophy of behavior that removed concepts of blame and punishment for vengeance sake. Hereditary and biologic causes of mental illness were combined with a new Freudian "psychic determinism," in which the crucial determinants of behavior were unconscious, to form a conceptual framework that absolved guilt and notions of wrongdoing [White 1923, 215-217; White 1938, 192]. Consequently, the defense experts may have believed that Thaw's actions were determined by events over which he had little control.

An obvious goal of the defense was to avoid prison for Thaw. Prison conditions in Thaw's day were appalling and abusive—places that could aggravate and cause mental illnesses [White 1923, 214-215; Krafft-Ebing, 156-157]. Individuals who were adjudicated mentally nonresponsible were treated more humanely in asylums than prisons. The result for society was considered the same by those seeking to reform sentencing laws. The "greater good" was protected in either case by isolating individuals who were dangerous. In fact, those found not guilty because of insanity stayed in asylums over two times longer than their counterparts in prison [White 1923, 222-225]. In addition, some psychiatrists felt a moral obligation to testify only for the defense in capital trials, because the job of a physician is to prolong life and not contribute to its destruction [White 1938, 191-192].

At least some of the criticism of the Thaw experts was due to inherent conflicts between medical and legal realms. Medical knowledge is derived from an analysis and weighing of facts, often obtained through discourse with colleagues with respect for different viewpoints. Among the medical specialties, psychiatry, especially, deals with subtle meanings and interpretations that involve numerous areas of gray. Many aspects of psychiatry are more closely related to the social sciences than the physical sciences. Consequently, it often does not stand up well in the heated, adversarial, black-and-white environment of the courtroom--where opinions are blocked and discredited without meaningful discussion. In addition, the adversarial nature of the courtroom means that experts with opposing opinions will testify, often providing entertaining copy for the media with their divergent views. Since experts receive payment for their testimonies, accusations regarding the "buying" of opinions are common.

Psychiatric testimony has been subject to criticism in almost every well-known legal case in which experts have voiced opinions. It is axiomatic that when legal insanity becomes an issue in the courtroom, psychiatry itself goes on trial. The psychiatrists for Thaw's defense were all respected leaders in their fields. Five were either past or future presidents of their national professional organizations, perhaps the highest honor that physicians bestow upon their peers. Commonsense infers they were men of integrity. If the experts and their opinions were on trial, it is reasonable to expect a presumption of innocence and the benefit of doubt regarding their ethics and motives.

Other Diagnostic Considerations

According to Nesbit, "extreme sadism" was one of the diagnoses given to Thaw, and it seems likely that Thaw would have met DSM criteria for "sexual sadism" [Nesbit, 166; DSM-IV-TR]. Individuals with sexual sadism have recurrent, intense sexual fantasies and behaviors that involve the infliction of psychological or physical suffering on unwilling participants.

Epilepsy, sometimes associated with impulsive aggression, was another diagnosis to be considered. However, other than a suspicion of seizures during Thaw's childhood, there was no reason to believe Thaw had epilepsy as an adult, and there is no record of epilepsy being diagnosed. There was no electroencephalogram (EEG) in 1907. Observation over time and an absence of physical signs and symptoms would have ruled out epilepsy as a diagnosis.

General paralysis (or paresis) of the insane must also have been considered in Thaw's differential diagnosis. General paralysis, i.e., cerebral neurosyphilis, produced many symptoms found in other disorders: euphoria, impaired judgment, memory loss, decreased ability to work, fatigue, progressive dementia and paranoid delusions [Dercum]. The relationship between primary syphilis and its tertiary forms, including general paralysis, was strongly suspected at the time of Thaw's trial, but it was not conclusively established until several years later [Hurd]. In 1906, a serum antibody test, the Wassermann test, became available as a test for syphilis [Wagner 1917].

General paralysis was responsible for nearly 10 percent of patients who were institutionalized in mental hospitals in the early 1900s, and it would not likely have been overlooked by the many specialists who examined Thaw. In fact, Wagner, who performed a detailed examination for the defense, published an article on general paralysis in the *American Journal of Insanity* in 1902 [Wagner 1902]. A careful history, Thaw's young age, physical examination, observation, and the Wassermann test would most likely have been used to eliminate neurosyphilis as a cause of Thaw's symptoms.

Final Speculation: Thaw's Symptoms in Current Terminology

The following summary of Thaw's symptoms in DSM-IV-TR nomenclature is highly speculative. However, on the basis of available information, a reasonable assumption is that Thaw had a pervasive developmental disorder of childhood, such as autistic or Asperger's disorder. As an adult, a high-functioning, autism-spectrum disorder could explain Thaw's unusual speech, poor social skills, and his eccentric and impulsive behavior. In addition, Thaw likely had a delusional, bipolar, or schizoaffective disorder. Of these, a delusional disorder, persecutory type, seems most probable. His clinical findings were likely complicated by cocaine abuse and dependency, which might explain some--but probably not all--of his symptoms. Thaw also likely met criteria for sexual sadism, and for a mixed personality disorder with narcissistic and antisocial features. Stressful events on the evening of the shooting could have combined to precipitate a dissociative or brief psychotic disorder, i.e., a "brain-storm."

Thaw was difficult to diagnose in his time, and would represent a diagnostic challenge today. Several psychiatrists would likely examine Thaw today and arrive at several different diagnoses. Psychiatric diagnosis is not an exact science. There is a lack of clear diagnostic boundaries between psychiatric disorders, and patients with multiple symptoms are often diagnosed with a multiple disorders [Regier et al.]. Consequently, as mentioned, some forensic experts discourage diagnosis in courtroom testimony [Morse]. For example, even with the availability of the DSM-III, experts in the 1982 insanity trial of John Hinckley, Jr., made 12 different diagnoses, many of them not found in the DSM--such as schizophrenic spectrum disorder, process schizophrenia, simple schizophrenia, pseudoneurotic schizophrenia and ambulatory schizophrenia (Stone, 84).

Chapter 7

THAW'S ONGOING LEGAL BATTLES

After his second trial, Thaw was committed to an asylum for the criminally insane, but he was not out of the news. His attorneys almost immediately filed a writ of habeas corpus stating that Thaw was no longer insane and asking the court to release him. This was denied, but over the next 7 years a deluge of writs were filed. Flint, one of the prosecution experts in the first trial, referred to the Thaw case as a "striking example of the misuse of the writ of habeas corpus" in a 1910 *American Journal of Insanity* article advocating reform of this procedure. Flint was convinced Thaw was suffering from paranoia and was incurable [Flint].[42]

Diagnoses given Thaw at release hearings included "chronic delusive [sic] insanity or paranoia" and "constitutional inferiority" [Mackenzie, 260, 265]. At a 1912 hearing, Adolf Meyer, M.D., was identified as Thaw's "principal alienist." Meyer at the time was chair of the department of psychiatry at Johns Hopkins University in Baltimore and presumably was employed privately as Thaw's psychiatrist.[43] The *Times* reported that Meyer "reluctantly" gave Thaw's diagnosis as "constitutional inferiority." W. A. White declined to elaborate on this diagnosis, stating it was not in use at his hospital (the Government Hospital for the Insane) [NYT 7/11/1912, 5].

---

42 Nesbit described a friendship with the elderly Flint that developed after the trials, "spending pleasant hours in his company" at a German beer hall. Since Flint frequently testified against Thaw at release hearings, this was upsetting to Thaw [Nesbit, 125].

43 Meyer was a consultant for Thaw since at least 1909, when he was director of the Pathological Institute for New York State Hospitals and professor of psychiatry at Cornell University [NYT 8/19/1909, 2; Winters]. Meyer was a long-term consultant for other wealthy clients, some from as far away as California, which at times required lengthy absences from Johns Hopkins [Scull, 161-163].

Thaw's efforts at release were rejected, but in March 1913 Thaw walked away from Matteawan in a planned escape and was taken across the border to Sherbrooke, Quebec Province, in Canada. He was given a hero's welcome in Canada with applauding "fans" lining the streets. His attorneys successfully fought extradition until he was returned to New York in December 1914.[44] Shortly afterwards, he was determined to be sane and released to the community on July 15, 1915 [Mooney, 272-273].

[44] Thaw's efforts to fight extradition went all the way to the U.S. Supreme Court. Thaw's attorneys argued that extradition rules should not apply because Thaw had not broken any laws by escaping from Matteawan because if he was insane, he should not be held accountable for his actions; and if he was sane, he should have been released. Justice Oliver Wendell Holmes, Jr., gave the opinion that while this argument might have validity in a trial, it was not pertinent to an extradition hearing, and Thaw was ordered back to New York from New Hampshire where he had been temporarily detained [Drew v Thaw].

Chapter 8

EVOLVING CONCEPTS OF "BRAIN-STORM" AND TEMPORARY INSANITY

"Temporary insanity" is not a precise concept. It is not a clear concept today and was probably less clear during the time of Thaw's trials. In 1907 "insanity" had both medical and legal meanings; today it is only a legal definition.

Jurors in the Thaw trial had to be confused to hear experts for the prosecution testify that Thaw was insane in the medical sense, i.e., having a serious mental illness; while not insane in the legal sense, i.e., he was responsible for his actions. In addition, it was difficult to comprehend how a person could be legally sane before an act was committed; legally insane during the act; and then sane shortly afterwards.

Early alienists described "homicidal impulses" in the context of moral insanity and questioned whether such impulses relieved an individual of criminal responsibility.

Samuel Woodward, M.D., the first president of the APA and one of its founders, raised the question of criminal responsibility in an 1845 case of homicidal impulse, where an individual retained the capacity of knowing right from wrong but could not control his actions [Woodward]. The concept of moral insanity became highly controversial, particularly when used in the insanity defense [Dain, 73-81; Zilboorg 1944, 550-552].

At the beginning of the 20th century, a variety of diagnostic entities were available to bolster a claim of temporary insanity. These included moral insanity, moral mania [Ray 1838, 168-170], homicidal insanity and homicidal monomania [Ray 1838, 213-234], homicidal impulse [Woodward], impulse insanity [Campbell, 579], inhibitory insanity [Zilboorg 1944, 551], transitory insanity and transitory mania [Krafft-Ebing, 206-210], maniacal furor [NYT 3/19/1907, 1], paroxysmal insanity [Spiegel and Spiegel], homicidal mania [NYT 3/1/1907, 2], emotional insanity [Chapin], psychokinesia [Campbell, 579] and "brain-storm." Other medical conditions could also cause temporary insanity, such as brain lesions, various forms of epilepsy and a number of physiologic and metabolic disturbances, such as delirium.

In retrospect, looking at the myriad of poorly defined diagnoses, "brain-storm" was in some respects a suitable term.[45] It was in words understood by nonprofessionals rather than esoteric medical jargon; it described a phenomenon that began and ended abruptly; it had some recognition in the medical literature; and it implied electrical activity in the brain that suggested a physical cause. In 1907 (and for many years before) most experts regarded insanity as a disease of the brain with physical causes [Dain, 84-85; Krafft-Ebing, 246; Rutter, 7-8].

With the development of psychoanalytic principles in the first part of the 20th century, unconscious mental conflicts became an explanation for violent outbursts. In 1937, Fredric Wertham introduced the phrase "catathymic crisis" to explain the sudden and explosive acting out of internal tensions arising from psychological conflicts. According to Wertham, after the release of internal tension there was a reintegration of defenses with a periodic return to normal functioning [Wertham]. In the 1960s, Karl Menninger described similar episodes of violence resulting from a breakdown of normal controls and inhibitions—something he termed "ego rupture" [Menninger, 226-229].

Among "official" diagnoses for episodic violence in the DSM (Diagnostic and Statistical Manual), "passive-aggressive personality, aggressive type" in DSM-I (1952) was applied to individuals for whom temper outbursts and destructive behavior were a frequent response to frustration. "Explosive personality disorder" (also called *epileptoid personality disorder*) was listed in the DSM-II (1968) for individuals who experienced unusual outbursts of rage and aggressiveness. "Intermittent explosive disorder" and "isolated explosive disorder" (described in the DSM as an equivalent of *catathymic crisis*) were introduced in the DSM-III (1980). "Isolated explosive disorder" was dropped from future manuals, but "intermittent explosive disorder," referring to

[45] In 1917, the APA adopted a classification for use in statistics; and there were collaborations with the National Committee for Mental Hygiene and the New York Academy of Medicine in the 1930s to establish diagnostic categories [DSM-I, v-xi]. But it wasn't until after World War II that a standard nomenclature was developed for clinical purposes in the first *Diagnostic and Statistical Manual [of] Mental Disorders* (DSM-I), published by the APA in 1952.

discrete episodes of aggression in the absence of impulsivity or aggressiveness between episodes, was retained and is included in the DSM-IV-TR (2000). However, the requirement for absence of inter-episode impulsivity was eliminated.

Other current DSM-IV-TR diagnoses—under certain circumstances—can be used to support the notion of temporary insanity. These include brief psychotic disorder, acute stress disorder, posttraumatic stress disorder, dissociative disorders, substance-related disorders including intoxication and withdrawal, personality disorders, attention-deficit/hyperactivity disorder, postpartum-related conditions, and even certain sleep disorders. Episodic violence can also occur in individuals with schizophrenia and other psychotic disorders, and with major mood disorders, especially during manic states [Sachs; Krakowski and Czobor].

Assaultive behavior can also occur with other medical conditions causing brain dysfunction and affective dysregulation, such as brain tumors, cerebral infections, delirium, cerebrovascular disorders, dementias, head injuries, and endocrine and metabolic conditions. In fact, virtually any medical and psychiatric condition can--and most likely has been used to--explain a loss of personal responsibility resulting in violent behavior. One of the more famous instances was the claim of metabolic temporary insanity in the 1979 "Twinkie defense" of Dan White for the murders of San Francisco Mayor George Moscone and City Supervisor Harvey Milk. Attorneys argued that the high carbohydrate content of food eaten by White caused a chemical imbalance that impaired his ability to control his behavior. The jury regarded this as a mitigating circumstance and returned a manslaughter verdict rather than murder [Dershowitz, 339]. Harvard attorney Alan M. Dershowitz described a number of similar "mental state" defenses in his 1994 book *The Abuse Excuse* (Little Brown and Co.).

The "storm" concept, however, lives on in terms such as "affective storms," for outbursts of anger and emotion [Koenigsberg; Davis; Goodman et al.]; and the neuroendocrine expression "dopamine storms" for psychotic episodes [Siris].

Chapter 9

FOLLOW-UP

Two years after his release from Matteawan, Thaw was arrested in Pittsburgh in 1917 on charges of kidnapping and whipping a 19-year-old male youth into unconsciousness. Thaw was again declared insane and committed to the Pennsylvania Hospital for the Insane in Philadelphia,[46] where he remained for the next seven years until his release in 1924 [NYT 6/13/24, 17; Mooney, 274-275]. In 1928 he was barred from entering England after being listed as an "undesirable"; and in the late 30s, he was sued for having beaten a nightclub hostess [NYT 6/7/28, 1; Baker, 396-397]. He later moved to Miami, where he died of a heart attack on Feb. 21, 1947, at age 76 [NYT 2/23/47, 53; Mooney, 275].

On Oct. 25, 1910, Evelyn Nesbit gave birth to a son, naming him Russell William Thaw. She maintained Thaw was the father and that he was conceived during one of her visits to Matteawan, where Thaw seemed to enjoy privileges denied other patients. Thaw denied paternity and did not contribute to his support [Uruburu, 363, 370]. In 1913 she returned to show business in a dance act with an English dancer, Jack Clifford. They had successful tours to sell-out audiences in the U.S. and Europe. When Thaw was released from Matteawan in 1915, Nesbit and Thaw promptly divorced, and she married Clifford a few months later. They separated after several years [Mooney, 287-295].

Nesbit made several silent films--including one in 1918 with her young son, Russell, titled *I Want to Forget* (Fox Films). No prints of her films are known to have survived. Gradually, her popularity faded. News stories

46 The Pennsylvania Hospital, the first hospital in Colonial America to provide treatment for the mentally ill, was founded in 1752. Benjamin Franklin had an instrumental role in its conception [Barton, 22].

appeared of suicide attempts and drug addiction [Los Angeles Herald 1/3/26, 1]. She was arrested in Panama on charges of gambling in 1929 [Mooney, 297]. In 1934 she wrote an autobiography, *Prodigal Days: The Untold Story*--an updated version of one written in 1914 [Nesbit]. She had several attempted comebacks, one at a New York nightclub in 1937, at the age of 52 [Baker, 397].

In 1955 she received $50,000 as a consultant for a movie of her life, *The Girl in the Red Velvet Swing* (20th Century-Fox). The title was taken from a swing that Stanford White had in one of his apartments that developed a reputation as place of seduction. Actress Joan Collins portrayed Nesbit. Nesbit moved to California, where she studied world religions and taught sculpturing at a local school [Mooney, 298; Lessard, 304]. She entered a nursing home in Santa Monica and died on Jan. 17, 1967, at the age of 82 [NYT 1/19/67, 1].

During Thaw's first trial, attorneys unsuccessfully tried to get Nesbit to say she despised White. In her testimony she said, "As a friend there was nobody I could think of nicer that Stanford White, outside the one act of his" [Baker, 389]. In her autobiography, she declared, "Right or wrong, I had loved Stanford White" [Nesbit, 109]. During an interview in the 1960s, she was quoted as saying, "Stanny was lucky. He died. I lived" [Mooney, 298].

Following Stanford White's death, stories emerged of lewd parties and secret rendezvous' he arranged at several of his apartment-studios in New York City.[47] The parties were attended by some of New York's most prominent businessmen, artists and politicians [Collins, 64-71; Mooney, 236-239]. One of the apartments contained the "red velvet swing" mentioned above. The most famous apartment occupied the top floor of Madison Square Garden, which White designed, where guests could leave his ornately decorated rooms and climb a circular staircase to touch the foot of the statue Diana, high above city lights [Nesbit, 18; Baker, 165-166]. After White's death, former associates distanced themselves from his reputation as stories circulated about wealthy, powerful men who preyed upon young girls coming to New York in hopes of careers [Mooney, 231-232]. While White was working in Manhattan, his wife, Bessie[48]--who married him in 1884--spent much of her time at their country home on Long Island [Mooney, 168].

47 According to some sources, the coy invitation to seduction "come up and see my etchings" had its origin in White's lofts [Lessard, 280].

48 The brother of Bessie Smith White, James Clinch Smith, perished on the Titanic the morning of April 15, 1912 [NYT 6/26/1912, 9]. Accounts of the tragedy described him as assisting the ship's second officer, Charles H. Lightoller, in loading women and children into lifeboat no. 4 [Butler, 127].

In 1996 Suzannah Lessard, a great-granddaughter of White, wrote *The Architect of Desire: Beauty and Danger in the Stanford White Family* (Delta Books). She, of course, never knew White, but she has fond recollections of her great-grandmother Bessie, who lived until Lessard was 6 [Lessard, 35-36]. Lessard believes that White's biggest flaw was a preoccupation with beauty in all forms: "Stanford consumed beauty and it consumed him" [Lessard, 120]. She described sexual excesses on his behalf and believed he was in the "grip of compulsions" with predetermined consequences [Lessard, 220]. However, she doesn't mince words when she accuses her great-grandfather of what was essentially a double rape of Nesbit: "[I]t was statutory rape because the age of consent was eighteen, and it was moral rape because Stanford was immeasurably more powerful than she was and a benefactor" [Lessard, 284]. Autopsy findings revealed White had fatty degeneration of the liver, kidney disease (Bright's disease) and "incipient tuberculosis." Lessard believes he would have died of natural causes within a year [Lessard, 219].

CONCLUSION

The 1907 trial of Harry Thaw was the first celebrity trial of the 20th century to utilize the insanity plea. Thaw's defense combined notions of temporary insanity with the "unwritten law." His first trial ended with a deadlocked jury, but a second trial found him not guilty by reason of insanity.

To bolster the concept of temporary insanity in his first trial, the defense diagnosed Thaw with a "brain-storm" on the night of the shooting. The concept of a brain-storm was ridiculed by the press and public; and criticized by legal and medical experts. District Attorney William Jerome called it the "paranoia of the millionaire." During a competency hearing, Jerome's own experts diagnosed Thaw with paranoia ("delusional disorder" in today's terminology), a diagnosis considered incurable with treatments of the time.

During Thaw's two trials, his mental health history was presented. This history revealed a troubled childhood and youth. Although speculative, Thaw may have had a pervasive developmental disorder of childhood, such as autistic or Asperger's disorder, and high-functioning, autism-spectrum disorder as an adult. It is also probable that he had a delusional, bipolar or schizoaffective disorder. Of these, a delusional disorder, persecutory type, seems most likely. A "wild card" in his differential diagnosis was cocaine abuse and dependency, which might have mimicked bipolar and paranoid symptoms. Sexual sadism and a mixed personality disorder with antisocial and narcissistic features were also likely.

It is also possible that Thaw experienced a "brain-storm," or brief psychotic disorder, on the evening of the shooting. Brain-storm, a layperson's term, described symptoms that could occur with other conditions. With no standard terminology in 1907, the much-maligned brain-storm diagnosis was in some respects an appropriate term to describe a sudden, drastic, temporary defect of reasoning having a physical cause.

Although experts for the defense were severely criticized and accused of "prostituting" their opinions, they were all leaders in their fields and, presumably, men of integrity. Five were either past or future presidents of their professional national organizations—the APA and ANA. While they may have been influenced by financial considerations, it was equally possible they were motivated by professional concerns regarding underutilization of the insanity defense, philosophical opinions regarding societal needs for imprisonment and punishment, and a moral obligation to preserve life whenever possible. They likely found themselves in an ethical dilemma by Thaw's insistence to waive a traditional insanity plea, resulting in the "brain-storm" defense. Part of their criticism was also due to inherent conflicts between medical and legal realms. Whenever legal insanity is raised in the courtroom, it can be expected that psychiatry itself will go on trial.

Temporary insanity was, and remains, an imprecise concept. Over the past century and a half, diagnostic entities encompassing this concept have included moral insanity, homicidal impulse, catathymic crisis, ego rupture, isolated explosive disorder, and brief psychotic disorder, to mention a few. Virtually any condition that causes temporary brain dysfunction and affective dysregulation can produce violent behavior consistent with this concept.

The strategy of the defense in Thaw's first trial, however, relied less upon diagnosis and the finer points of insanity law, and more upon gaining sympathy for the defendant and creating doubt regarding his sanity. By exposing jurors to a "war of the experts" and subsequent legal arguments, the defense hoped to reshape jurors' concepts of the relationships between insanity, justifiable homicide, and the right of a husband to avenge dishonor for himself and his wife. This strategy met with some success because the jury did not return a murder verdict. Similar strategies are in use today.

REFERENCES

Ackerman, R. H. (1992). Graeme M. Hammond and the ANA. *Annals of Neurology, 32*, 224.

Abbot, E. S. (1914). What is paranoia? *American Journal of Insanity, 71*, 29-40.

Abell, F., and Hare, D .J. (2005). An experimental investigation of the phenomenology of delusional beliefs in people with Asperger syndrome. *Autism, 9*, 515-531.

American Psychiatric Association (APA) (2001). *AMA Principles of Medical Ethics with Annotations Especially Applicable to Psychiatry.* Washington DC: American Psychiatric Association.

Baker, P. R. (1989). *Stanny: The Gilded Life of Stanford White*. New York: Macmillan.

Bardwell, M. C., and Arrigo, B. A. (2002). *Criminal Competency on Trial: the Case of Colin Ferguson.* Durham NC: Carolina Academic Press.

Barton, W. E. (1987). The *History and Influence of the American Psychiatric Association*. Washington DC: American Psychiatric Association.

Berrios, G. E., and Freeman, H. (1991). *150 Years of British Psychiatry, 1841-1991*. London: Royal College of Psychiatrists.

Bouvier, J. (1897). *Bouvier's Law Dictionary, vol. 1*. Boston: Boston Book Co.

Brigham, A. (1847). Crime and insanity. *American Journal of Insanity, 4*, 67-72.

Bryant, R. H. (1927). The constitutional psychopathic inferior: a menace to society and a suggestion for the disposition of such individuals. *American Journal of Psychiatry, 87*, 671-689.

Buchanan, A. (2006). Psychiatric evidence on the ultimate issue. *Journal of the American Academy of Psychiatry and the Law, 34*, 14-21.

Bunker, H. A. (1944). American psychiatry as a specialty. In J. K. Hall (Ed.), *One Hundred Years of American Psychiatry* (pp. 479-505). New York: Columbia University.

Burnham, J. C. (1967). *Psychoanalysis and American Medicine: 1894-1918. Psychological Issues, Monograph 20.* New York: International Universities.

Burnham, J. C. (1983). *Jelliffe: American Psychoanalyst and Physician: His Correspondence with Sigmund Freud and C.G. Jung*. Chicago: University of Chicago.

Butler, D. A. (2002). *"Unsinkable": The Full Story of the RMS Titanic.* Cambridge MA: Da Capo Press.

Campbell, R. J. (1996). *Psychiatric Dictionary*, 7th edition. New York: Oxford University.

Caplan, L. (1987). *The Insanity Defense and the Trial of John W. Hinckley, Jr.* New York: Dell Books.

Chapin, J. B. (1909).The insanity defense for crime. *American Journal of Insanity, 66*, 71-82.

Chusid, J. G. (1973). *Correlative Neuroanatomy and Functional Neurology.* Los Altos, CA: Lange Medical Publications.

Chapman, R. L. (1998). *American Slang.* New York: Harper Collins.

Clarke, D., Baxter, M., Perry, D., and Prahser, V. (1999). The diagnosis of affective and psychotic disorders in adults with autism: seven case reports. *Autism, 3*, 149-164.

Clarke, D. J., Littlejohns, C. S., Corbett, J. A., and Joseph, S. (1989). Pervasive developmental disorders and psychoses in adult life. *British Journal of Psychiatry*, 155, 692-699.

Clouston, T. S. (1904). *Clinical Lectures on Mental Diseases*, 6th edition. New York: Lea Brothers and Co. Online at Google Book Search, http://books.google.com. Accessed 12/17/2008.

Cobb, I. S. (1942). *Exit Laughing*. Garden City NY: Garden City Pub.

Collins, F. L. (1932). *Glamorous Sinners*. New York: Long and Smith.

Dain, N. (1964). *Concepts of Insanity in the United States, 1789-1865*. New Brunswick NJ: Rutgers University.

Davis, R. E. (1979). Manic-depressive variant syndrome of childhood: a preliminary report. *American Journal of Psychiatry, 136*, 702-706.

Dercum, F. X. (1902). The early diagnosis of paresis. *American Journal of Insanity, 58*, 575-585.

Dershowitz, A. M. (1994). *The Abuse Excuse*. Boston: Little Brown and Co.

Deutsch, A. (1949). *The Mentally Ill in America*. New York: Columbia University Press.

Diagnostic and Statistical Manual [of] Mental Disorders. (1952). 1st edition (DSM-I). Washington DC: American Psychiatric Association.

Diagnostic and Statistical Manual of Mental Disorders. (1968). 2nd edition (DSM-II). Washington, DC: American Psychiatric Association.

Diagnostic and Statistical Manual of Mental Disorders. (1980). 3rd edition (DSM-III). Washington DC: American Psychiatric Association.

Diagnostic and Statistical Manual of Mental Disorders. (1987). 3rd edition, Revised (DSM-III-R). Washington DC: American Psychiatric Association.

Diagnostic and Statistical Manual of Mental Disorders. (2000). 4th edition, Text Revision (DSM-IV-TR). Washington DC: American Psychiatric Association.

Drew v Thaw, 235 U.S. 432 (1914).

Drew, C. A. (1904). Was he a paranoic? *American Journal of Insanity, 60*, 611-633.

Dewey, R. (1904). Apparent recovery in a case of paranoia. *American Journal of Insanity, 60*, 443-339.

Editorial (1907). Defense of insanity in criminal cases and medical expert testimony. *American Lawyer, 15*, 309.

Editorial (1934). Comments on honor defense and insanity plea. *Yale Law Journal, 43*, 809-814.

Eigen, J. P. (1999). Lesions of the will: medical resolve and criminal responsibility in Victorian insanity trials. *Law and Society Review, 33*, 425-459.

Esquirol, J. E. D. (1845). *Mental Maladies: A Treatise on Insanity*. New York: Hafner Pub. Reprint edition, 1965.

Evans, B. D. (1909). Court testimony of alienists. *American Journal of Insanity, 66*. 83-109.

Freud, S. (1910). Contributions to the psychology of love, a special type of choice of object made by men, in *Collected Papers*, Vol. 4, (1959). New York: Basic Books.

Freud, S. (1911-1913). Schreber—Psychoanalytic notes on an autobiographical account of a case of paranoia (dementia paranoides) (1911-1913). In J. Strachey (Ed.), *The Complete Psychological Works,* Vol. 12. (1955). London: Hogarth Press.

Finkel, N. J. (1988). *Insanity on Trial*. New York: Plenum.

Flint, A. (1910). Methods of dealing with the criminal insane—defects in present methods and suggested remedies. *American Journal of Insanity, 67*, 227-240.

Friedman, L. M. (1993). *Crime and Punishment in American History*. New York: Basic Books.

Goodman, M., Hazlett, E. A., New, A. S., et al. (2009). Quieting the affective storm of borderline personality disorder. *American Journal of Psychiatry,166*, 522-528.

Gould, G. M. (1894). *An Illustrated Dictionary of Medicine, Biology and Allied Sciences*. Philadelphia: P. Blakiston, Son and Co.

Gould, G. M. (1907). *An Illustrated Dictionary of Medicine, Biology and Allied Sciences*. Philadelphia: P. Blakiston Son and Co. Online at http://www.archive.org/details/illustrateddict100gouluoft.. Accessed 3/31/09.

Hamilton, A. M., and Grasset, J. The intimate relation of genius to insanity: *The New York Times*, 3/31/1907, SM5.

Hamilton, A. M. (1907). An expert's view. *American Lawyer, 15*, 311.

Hamilton, A. M. (1916). *Recollections of an Alienist: Personal and Professional*. New York: George H. Doran Co. Online at Google Book Search, http://books.google.com. Accessed 12/02/2008.

Haskins, B. G., and Silva, J. A. (2006). Asperger's disorder and criminal behavior: forensic-psychiatric considerations. *Journal of the American Academy of Psychiatry and the Law, 34,* 374-384.

Herbel, B. L., and Stelmach, H. (2007). Involuntary medication treatment for competency restoration of 22 defendants with delusional disorder. *Journal of the American Academy of Psychiatry and the Law, 35*, 47-59.

Hill, G. H. (1900). Dementia praecox. *American Journal of Insanity, 57*, 319-324.

Hurd, A. W. (1902). Etiology of paresis. *American Journal of Insanity, 58*, 565-574.

Ireland, R. M. (1988). Insanity and the unwritten law. *American Journal of Legal History, 32*, 157-172.

Jacoby, G. W. (1907). Psychiatric expert evidence in criminal proceedings: its imperfections and remedy. *New York Medical Journal, 87*, 431-437.

Jacoby, G. W. (1918). *The Unsound Mind and the Law: A Presentation of Forensic Psychiatry*. New York: Funk and Wagnalls.

Keedy, E. R. (1917). Insanity and criminal responsibility II. *Harvard Law Review, 30*, 731.

Keedy, E. R. (1952). Irresistible impulse as a defense in the criminal law. *University Pennsylvania Law Review, 100*, 977-979.

Knappman, E. W. (Ed.) (2002). *Great American Trials: Vol 1: 1637-1949.* New York: New England Publishing.

Koenigsberg, H. W. (1994). The combination of psychotherapy and pharmacotherapy in the treatment of borderline patients. *Journal of Psychotherapy Practice and Research, 3*, 93-107.

Kraeplin, E. (1901). A general view of dementia precox. Trans. by A. E. Brownrigg. *American Journal of Insanity, 58*, 121-132.

Krakowski, M., and Czobor, P. (1997). Violence in psychiatric patients: the role of psychosis, frontal lobe impairment, and ward turmoil. *Comprehensive Psychiatry, 38*, 230-236.

Krafft-Ebing, R. von. (1904). *Text-Book of Insanity Based on Clinical Observations for Practitioners and Students of Medicine.* Trans. C. G. Chaddock. Philadelphia: FA Davis.

Langford, G. (1962). *The Murder of Stanford White*. New York: Bobbs-Merrill Co.

Laughlin, H. P. (1970). *The Ego and Its Defenses*. New York: Appleton-Century-Crofts.

Lessard, S. (1996). *The Architect of Desire: Beauty and Danger in the Stanford White Family*. New York: Delta.

Little, M. (1992). William James and the noun *brainstorm*. *Notes and Queries, 39*, 187.

Longe, J. L., and D. S. Blanchfield (Eds.) (2002). *The Gale Encyclopedia of Medicine. 5 vols*. Detroit: Gale Group.

MacDonald, C. F. (1902). The trial, execution, autopsy and mental status of Leon F. Czolgosz, alias Fred Nieman, the assassin of President McKinley. *American Journal of Insanity, 58*, 369-386.

MacDonald,C. F. (1910). The ethical aspects of expert testimony in relation to the plea of insanity as a defense to an indictment for crime. *American Journal of Insanity 67*, 241-255.

Mackenzie, F. A. (1928). *The Trial of Harry Thaw*. London: Geoffrey Bles. reprint Holmes Beach FL: Gaunt, 2000.

McDonald, W. (1904). The present status of paranoia. *American Journal of Insanity, 60*, 475-494.

Mathes, J. L. (1971). The Madonna-prostitute syndrome. *Medical Aspects of Human Sexuality, 5*, 202-209.

Menninger, K. (1963). *The Vital Balance*. New York: Viking Press.

Meyer, A. (1903). Arrest of development of adolescence. Discussion after address of Dr. Stanley Hall, National Education Association meeting, July 1903. In E. E. Winters (Ed.), *The Collected Papers of Adolf Meyer* (1952). Vol. 2. (p. 418). Baltimore: Johns Hopkins Press.

Meyer, A. (1905). Movement for a change in statistics. Seventeenth Annual Report of the State Commission in Lunacy, Sept. 30, 1905. In E. E. Winters (Ed.), *The Collected Papers of Adolf Meyer* (1952). Vol. 2. (pp. 144-145). Baltimore: Johns Hopkins Press.

Meyer, A. (1912). The status of the medical and scientific work in the Massachusetts hospitals for the insane. Address delivered Feb. 7, 1912, in Boston before the Governor and Council of Massachusetts and the superintendents of the state institutions for the insane. In E. E. Winters (Ed.), *The Collected Papers of Adolf Meyer* (1952). Vol. 2. (p. 56). Baltimore: Johns Hopkins Press.

Meyer, A. (1928). Thirty-five years of psychiatry in the United States and our present outlook. *American Journal of Psychiatry, 85*, 1-31.

Ming, X., Julu, P. O., Brimacombe, M., et al. (2005). Reduced cardiac parasympathetic activity in children with autism. *Brain and Development, 27*, 509-516.

Mooney, M. M. (1976). *Evelyn Nesbit and Stanford White: Love and Death in the Gilded Age.* New York: W. Morrow.

Moore, L. C. (1976). William Alanson White—a biography (1870-1937). In A. R. D'Amore (Ed.), *William Alanson White: The Washington Years, 1903-1937: The Contributions to Psychiatry, Psychoanalysis and Mental Health by Dr. White While Superintendent of Saint Elizabeths Hospital.* (p. 15). Washington DC: DHEW.

Moran, R. (1981). *Knowing Right from Wrong: The Insanity Defense of Daniel McNaughtan.* New York: Free Press.

Morse, S. J. (2008). The ethics of forensic practice: reclaiming the wasteland. *Journal of the American Academy of Psychiatry and the Law, 36,* 206-217.

Morton,W. A. (1999). Cocaine and psychiatric symptoms. *The Primary Care Companion to the Journal of Clinical Psychiatry, 1*, 109-113.

Mossman, D., and Dunseith, N. W. (2001). "A fool for a client": print portrayals of 49 *pro se* criminal defendants. *Journal of the American Academy of Psychiatry and the Law, 29*, 408-419.

Mossman, D., Noffsinger, S. G., Ash, P., et al. (2007). Practice guidelines: forensic evaluation of competence to stand trial. *Journal of the American Academy of Psychiatry and the Law, 35* (Supplement 4): S6-S7.

Nesbit, E. (1934). *Prodigal Days: The Untold Story*. New York: J. Messner. Reprint D. D. Paul (Ed.), 2004.

Noll, R. (2007). Kraepelin's "lost biological psychiatry"? Autointoxication, organotherapy and surgery for dementia praecox. *History of Psychiatry, 18*, 301-319.

NYT: *The New York Times*, various dates as given in text.

O'Conner, R. (1963). *Courtroom Warrior: The Combative Career of William Travers Jerome*. Boston: Little, Brown and Co.

Osborne, J. W. (1907). A defense of the present system. *Americam Lawyer*, 15, 311-312.

Oxford English Dictionary (2001). Vol 2 (2nd edition). Oxford: Oxford University Press.

Page, C. W. (1904). Paranoid dementia. *American Journal of Insanity*, 60, 525-535.

Parsons, F. W. (1934). Charles W. Pilgrim. *American Journal of Psychiatry*, 91, 234-237.

Perlin, M. L. (1995). *Law and Mental Disability*. Charlottesville VA: Michie.

Pilgrim, C. W. (1911). The care and treatment of the insane in the state of New York. *American Journal of Insanity*, 1911, 68, 1-13.

Pinta, E. R. (2008). Examining Harry Thaw's "brain-storm" defense: APA and ANA presidents as expert witnesses in a 1907 trial. *Psychiatric Quarterly, 79*, 83-89.

Polk's Medical Register and Directory of North America. (1908). (10th edition). Chicago, R.L. Polk Co.

Rausch, J. L., Johnson, M. E., and Casanova, M. F. (2008). *Asperger's Disorder*. New York: Informa Health Care, pp. 279-280.

Ray, I. (1838). *A Treatise on the Medical Jurisprudence of Insanity*. Boston: Charles C. Little and James Brown.

Ray, I. (1861). An examination of the objections to the doctrine of moral insanity. *American Journal of Insanity, 18*, 112-138.

Regier, D. A., Narrow, W. E., Kuhl, E. A., and Kupfer, D. J. (2009). The conceptual development of DSM-V. *American Journal of Psychiatry, 166*, 645-650.

Robinson, D. N. (1996). *Wild Beasts and Idle Humours: The Insanity Defense from Antiquity to the Present.* Cambridge Mass: Harvard University.

Roth, L. M. (1983). *McKim, Mead and White, Architects*. New York: Harper and Row.

Rutter, H. C. (1905). *Manual of Insanity with Especial Reference to Criminal Responsibility*. Columbus OH: Midland.

Sachs, G. S. (2006). A review of agitation in mental illness: burden of illness and underlying pathology. *Journal of Clinical Psychiatry*, 67, (Supplement 10): 5-12.

Sadock, B. J., and V. A. Sadock (Ed.) (1999). *Kaplan and Sadock's Comprehensive Textbook of Psychiatry,* 2 Vol. Philadelphia: Lippincott, Williams and Wilkins.

Satel, S. L., Southwick, S. M., and Gawin, F. H. (1991). Clinical features of cocaine-induced paranoia. *American Journal of Psychiatry, 148*, 495-498.

Scull, A. (2005). *Madhouse: A Tragic Tale of Megalomania and Modern Medicine*. New Haven: Yale University Press.

Shapiro, D. (1965). *Neurotic Styles*. New York: Basic Books.

Shorter, E. (1997). *A History of Psychiatry: From the Era of the Asylum to the Age of Prozac*. New York: John Wiley and Sons.

Siris, S. G. (2000). Depression in schizophrenia: perspective in the era of "atypical" antipsychotic agents. *American Journal of Psychiatry, 157*, 1381.

Somerville, H. M. (1907). A judicial view. *American Lawyer, 15*, 309-10.

Spiegel, A. D., and Spiegel, M. S. (1991). Not guilty by reason of paroxysmal insanity: the "mad" doctor vs. "common sense" doctors in an 1865 trial. *Psychiatric Quarterly, 62*, 51-66.

Spiegel, A. D., and Suskind, P. B. (2000). Uncontrollable frenzy and a unique temporary insanity plea. *Journal of Community Health, 25*, 157-179.

Stark, E. J. (as Bud Manchester) (1907). *Brain-Storm Rag*. St. Louis: Stark Music Co.

State v Thompson, Wright's Ohio Rep 617 (1834)

Stedman, H. R., MacDonald, C. F., Mills, C. K.. et al. (1910). Report of the committee on medical expert testimony of the American Medico-Psychological Association. *American Journal of Insanity, 67*, 177-186.

Stone, A. A. (1984). *Law, Psychiatry and Morality: Essays and Analysis*. Washington DC: American Psychiatric Press.

Swanberg W.A. (1956). *Sickles the Incredible.* Gettysburg PA: Stan Clark. Reprint Charles Scribner's Sons, 1991.

Taber, C. W. (1993). *Taber's Cyclopedic Medical Dictionary* (17th edition). Philadelphia: FA Davis.

Thaw, H. K. (1926). *The Traitor*. Philadelphia: Dorrence.

Umphrey, M. M. (1999). Dialogics of legal meaning: spectacular trials, the unwritten law and narratives of criminal responsibility. *Law and Society Review, 33*, 393-423.

Uruburu, P. (2008). *American Eve: Evelyn Nesbit, Stanford White, the Birth of the "It" Girl and the Crime of the Century*. New York: Riverhead Books.

U.S. Department of Labor, Bureau of Labor Statistics, Consumer Price Index. Online at http://www.bls.gov/cpi/ Accessed 6/5/09.

Wagner, C. G. (1902). The comparative frequency of general paresis. *American Journal of Insanity, 58*, 587-595.

Wagner, C. G. (1917). Recent trends in psychiatry. *American Journal of Insanity, 74*, 1-14.

Wain, H. (1958). *The Story Behind the Word.* Springfield IL: Charles C. Thomas.

Wannarka, M. B. (1968). Dr. George Milbry Gould: ophthalmologist and first president of the Medical Library Association. *Bulletin of the History of Medicine, 42,* 265-271.

Wertham, F. (1937). The catathymic crisis. *Archives of Neurology and Psychiatry, 37*, 974-978.

White, W. A. (1907). *Outlines of Psychiatry. Nervous and Mental Disease Monograph Series No. 1*. New York: Journal of Nervous and Mental Disease Publishing Co.

White, W. A. (1908). Expert testimony and the alienist. *New York Medical Journal, 88*, 150-154.

White, W. A., and S. E. Jelliffe (Ed.) (1913). *The Modern Treatment of Nervous and Mental Diseases,* 2 Vol. Philadelphia: Lea and Febiger.

White, W. A., and Jelliffe, S. E. (1915). *Diseases of the Nervous System: A Text-Book of Neurology and Psychiatry*. Philadelphia: Lea and Febiger.

White, W. A. (1923). *Insanity and the Criminal Law*. New York: Macmillan Books.

White, W. A. (1938). *William Alanson White: The Autobiography of a Purpose*. New York: Doubleday, Doran and Co.

Winters, E. E. (Ed.) (1952) *The Collected Papers of Adolf Meyer*. (Vol. 3, p. 539). Baltimore: Johns Hopkins.

Woodbury, F. (1910). Brain storm. *New York Medical Journal, 91*, 531-534.

Woodward, S. B. (1845). Homicidal impulse. *American Journal of Insanity, 1*, 323-326.

Zilboorg G. (1941). *A History of Medical Psychology*. New York: W.W. Norton and Co.

Zilboorg G. (1944). Legal aspects of psychiatry. In J. K. Hall (Ed.), *One Hundred Years of American Psychiatry* (pp. 507-588). New York: Columbia University.

INDEX

A

B

C

D

E

F

G

H

I

J

K

L

M

Q

R

S